# MENTORING PROGRAMS

## THAT WORK

# JENN LABIN

PRESS

ATD Press is an internationally renowned source of insightful and practical information on talent development, training, and professional development.

ATD Press
1640 King Street
Alexandria, VA 22314 USA

Ordering information: Books published by ATD Press can be purchased by visiting ATD's website at www.td.org/books or by calling 800.628.2783 or 703.683.8100.

Library of Congress Control Number: 2017930321

ISBN-10: 1-56286-458-0
ISBN-13: 978-1-56286-458-3
e-ISBN: 978-1-60728-115-3

**ATD Press Editorial Staff**
Director: Kristine Luecker
Manager: Christian Green
Community of Practice Manager, Human Capital: Ann Parker
Senior Associate Editor: Melissa Jones
Text Design: Iris Sanchez
Cover Design: Faceout Studio

Printed by P.A. Hutchison Company, Mayfield, PA

# Contents

# Foreword

It is no secret that more organizations than ever are embracing mentoring. I use "embracing" advisedly because its pervasiveness and popularity is now undeniable. This groundswell of interest has generated the widespread acceptance of mentoring as a best practice and elevated it to the level of a strategic imperative.

There are many reasons for the increased interest and investment in mentoring:

- While Baby Boomers retire, the 80 million Millennials who are in or entering the workforce believe having a mentor will help them succeed. It is little wonder then that mentoring has become a vehicle for recruiting and retaining future talent.
- Emerging leaders are more likely to be loyal to an organization where they feel valued, and mentoring nurtures and deepens organizational commitment.
- Mentoring builds and strengthens the talent pipeline—it is a leadership competency. So, organizations are investing in leadership development to ensure smooth transitions and continuity of prepared leaders.
- Knowledge silos contribute to a lack of alignment, making it difficult to distribute knowledge evenly throughout the organization. Mentoring facilitates strategic alignment by facilitating and sharing knowledge.
- Mentoring promotes diversity and inclusion, giving everyone an opportunity to learn from the diversity within an organization.
- At the heart of mentoring is a profound personal benefit that goes beyond organizational value.
- Mentoring provides a safety to help and to guide mentees in their career development. By sharing experience and expertise, mentors help mentees avoid common pitfalls that slow or derail learning.
- Mentors help mentees develop the capability, confidence, and competence to accomplish their goals. Because they've "been there and done that," mentors are in a unique position to share what they've learned and help mentees understand the skills they need to be successful.

Achieving positive outcomes like these across a broad organizational context is impossible without a solid planning framework. But how do you get there?

If you are a learning and development specialist, talent manager, HR professional, mentoring program manager, or a member of a steering committee charged with launching, executing, and coordinating a mentoring program, you already know that developing a successful program can be a daunting and overwhelming task that takes dedicated time and effort. Unfortunately, time is something none of us has in abundance.

Fortunately, Jennifer Labin has written a primer that simplifies the process. With more than 15 years of experience as a program development specialist, she presents a framework to create sustainable programs that mentoring program managers can easily manage.

Known as the AXLES Framework for Developing Mentoring Programs, her process includes five individual, critical components that need to be planned and designed prior to launching your mentoring program. The five components are align, experience, launch, effectiveness, and support.

Achieving alignment is a priority for me when it comes to mentoring. Gaining momentum and forward traction is impossible without internal and external alignment, which is essential to promoting consistency of practice, cultural fit, and coordination. In addition, alignment maintains integrity and promotes ongoing effectiveness, and interdependence of functions, all while creating the momentum needed for ensuring organizational vitality, viability, and vibrancy. In short, it affects the functionality and effectiveness of mentoring programs. It requires vigilance and steadfastness.

*Mentoring Programs That Work* has the practical tools and best practices you need to create a well-implemented mentoring program. The step-by-step approach to program development integrates diagrams, images, case studies, examples, and key insights and exercises into a practical and culturally malleable process.

Poet Robert Creeley wrote:

> Here is
> where there
> is.

If you want to get to where there is, *Mentoring Programs That Work* begins here.

Lois Zachary
Phoenix, Arizona
February 2017

# Preface

I remember sitting in a frigid classroom at the ATD International Conference & Exposition many years ago watching my facilitator command total engagement from the room. She was passionate, driven, credible, talented, and challenging (in a good way)—a total powerhouse coming in at about 5 feet tall. I thought, I have to learn more from this woman.

So I asked Elaine Biech to be my mentor.

Over the course of my career, Elaine has pushed me to set my goals higher. She has fielded more than one of my calls when I was emotional and needed to process a professional stumble. Elaine encouraged me to not only write my first book, but this one as well. If I said to her, "I can't do it," she was always ready to ask, "Why not?"

Elaine is everything a person could want in a mentor; thanks to her, I now have firsthand experience of how a stellar mentor (as a role model, sponsor, and champion) can change the trajectory of a career.

I wanted to help others find the same kind of mentoring relationship I had with Elaine, so I began seeking ways to develop mentoring programs. However, rather than creating new, effective programs, I was repeatedly engaged to help organizations fix their "broken" programs, which were ineffective at best and poorly designed at worst.

There were common issues across these ineffective programs. Each emphasized a learning event, such as launching the program or matching the participants. None of them supported a sustained learning process or created a cohesive and supportive experience for learners and mentors.

So why did these programs fail? The practitioners who originally created them did everything right according to the ADDIE model of training design (or whichever model they followed). The problem was they were applying a training methodology to a nontraining solution.

While developing about two dozen different mentoring programs, I had the opportunity to create a unique approach—one that focused on the amazing benefits mentoring has over traditional training, as well as the risks associated with this unique developmental solution. The result was the AXLES model, which was created from hands-on, everyday, experimentation.

After I started sharing the AXLES approach with colleagues and saw how helpful they found it, the idea for this book began to take shape. It's still my mission to help others find dynamic mentors like mine. Writing this book and introducing the AXLES model to the world is the best way I have to empower people to create impactful mentoring programs.

In my journey I have benefited not only from Elaine's guidance, but from many others' as well. I'm not the first author to worry about forgetting to acknowledge someone, but I'll attempt to highlight a few. I continue to learn every day from mentors of the highest caliber. Thank you so much to Elaine Biech, Nancy Duarte, Charlie Gilkey, and Lou Russell for all you contribute to the world of training. I am infinitely grateful for everything you have taught me.

I am also grateful to an amazing group of clients and partners with whom I get to work and learn from every day. Big, thankful hugs go out to Laura Wall Klieves, Kevin Friesen, Eric Albertson, and the whole Duarte Academy team. I am also thankful to Randy Emelo, George Hallenbeck, Davida Sharpe, and Floyd Carlson, who have been partners, thought leaders, and contributors as I strive to get the word out about mentoring.

I also want to thank Michael Lee Stallard, Jeanne Masseth, and Jean Williams, who have been so generous to contribute to this book. So much gratitude also goes to Wendy and Jim Kirkpatrick who have not only given their time to this book, but have also been champions and mentors for me for a number of years.

The work we do at TERP associates involves a team of people who wear different hats depending on our clients' needs. We would not be able to deliver such results to our clients without Diana, Jax, Megan, Insoo, and the rest of the TERP family. Thank you!

This brings me to Kelly Irons, my business partner and other half of my brain. There just aren't enough words to express everything I have learned from you. You are an incredible mentor.

And last, but never least, I am grateful beyond measure for my family. Jon, Zoë, and Aria, you are more supportive than I could ever hope for, and more amazing than I could ever dream of. You are my daily inspiration.

With much gratitude,
Jenn Labin

# Introduction

Mentoring is set apart from other types of talent development by one simple fact: Mentoring relationships are highly impactful. They drive results, challenge talent, and change careers for the better. The following are some typical experiences talent development practitioners have had in their own mentoring relationships:

> "My mentors have given me perspective when it was most critical, security that I'm never far from wise counsel, and inspiration to pass on that same gift to others. What other investment yields such rewards?"
>
> —Kevin Friesen, Duarte

> "Mentoring has been an integral part of my development and growth, both professionally and personally. My experience with mentoring has opened doors as well as my eyes to all sorts of opportunities."
>
> —Crystal Richards, Principal, Mosaic Resource Group

> "Mentoring has been one of the primary pillars of my career. Without the guidance, perspective, and insight from more tenured partners in my field, I would not be where I am today."
>
> —Jacqueline Geary, Talent Development Analyst, Aerotek

These positive real-life experiences are corroborated by research on the effect of mentoring. For example, the Corporate Leadership Council (2005) found that "'feedback and relationships programs' [such as mentoring] outrank 'experience-based' and 'education-based' development programs." And, in its publication

*Best Practices: Mentoring*, the U.S. Office of Personnel Management (2008) noted that, "From increased morale to increased organizational productivity and career development, the benefits of an organization that actively supports mentoring are numerous."

Randy Emelo highlights mentoring's ability to create an innovative, "nimble workforce that can adapt to rapid change, new demands, and unforeseen challenges" in his book, *Modern Mentoring* (2008). He goes on to emphasize how critical it is to provide ways for employees "to connect, collaborate, learn from, and share with their colleagues across all levels, locations, and functions."

Finally, Linda Phillips-Jones (2003) writes in *The Mentor's Guide* that "powerful things happen when a respected, experienced person shows interest in and goes out of his/her way to help another individual develop, especially when that individual is open to being influenced."

But, if everyone agrees that mentoring is so valuable, why doesn't every organization have an effective mentoring program? Proving the value of mentoring is not the problem. The real issue is the plethora of ineffective formal mentoring programs, which fail because of poor alignment, unskilled mentors, or lack of leadership champions for the programs, or because the programs aren't sustainable or scalable.

## Creating an Effective Mentoring Program

Organizations may set out intending to build valuable and effective solutions, but if practitioners can't visualize the why and how of mentoring programs, they will fail.

The disciplines of instructional design and talent development teach you how to build classroom training and e-learning programs. But developing mentoring programs requires a different set of skills. Talent development practitioners are involved in numerous development and launch projects over their career, which gives them the opportunity to develop and refine techniques that work in different situations. However, an organization might only implement a single mentoring program, or maybe a couple across a larger organization. Thus, few practitioners have the opportunity to find out which choices work best in different mentoring applications. In addition, it's often challenging to figure out what might work when developing formal mentoring programs, without having a map or stakeholders to act as champions for the program. While there are many models for building training, nothing specifically addresses the unique aspects of how to build a successful mentoring program.

Classroom-based learning provides ample opportunities to see progress and challenges firsthand. Virtual training (for example, over web-conferencing software) also uses real-time cues to let facilitators and program administrators change course in their techniques, if necessary. Even e-learning is highly tracked and observable.

Mentoring programs are different because learning happens "out there"—away from classrooms, webcams, and learning management systems. In a mentoring relationship, there is usually a mentor (a more experienced individual providing guidance and support) and at least one learner (a less experienced individual seeking guidance and support). This dynamic creates a sharp contrast from the traditional one-to-many classroom model, and thus has its own benefits, challenges, and measurability.

## Benefits of a Successful Mentoring Program

Because mentors can address whatever the learner needs in the moment, without having to focus on predetermined content, learners can enhance their skills and knowledge in a variety of areas and have the flexibility to explore topics with the greatest urgency and importance. In one mentoring conversation, a learner might enhance her confidence in presentations, and in the next, she might focus on strategies for product marketing.

In addition, because learners are able to get the guidance they need from their mentors when they need it, there is greater applicability. For example, during a mentoring conversation, a learner might ask for direction about how to approach an executive about a new project. The mentor might provide some ideas, and use interactive questioning to help the learner brainstorm other ideas. The learner now has an action plan, and could meet with the executive that afternoon. He may also connect with his mentor the following week to discuss how the meeting went and get follow-up advice.

Mentoring programs create a learning environment that is more sustainable than many training solutions because it is based on connections between people instead of events. Development that results from mentoring is likely to last, in part, because mentoring relationships are often nurtured and longer lasting. Continual reinforcement over the course of a mentoring relationship ensures that learners are aware of their progress and can seek ways to apply their increased skills.

## Challenges of a Successful Mentoring Program

Mentoring programs also come with their own challenges. The most important difference between mentoring programs and training is that the success of the mentoring program hinges on the participant experience. Program developers must anticipate how to create the right amount of structure and support for the organization, whereas program administrators have to be responsive to the ongoing needs of their learners and mentors.

A program developed with a lot of structure, rigid requirements, multiple check-ins, and frequent participant surveys will fail in an organization that thrives on innovation and a collaborative work environment. Conversely, informal programs with very little in the way of communication or administrative support will fail in more traditional and hierarchical organizations.

Because mentoring programs are not typically based on prescribed content, new and unique requests constantly arise during their life cycle. Administrators may be called upon to create new job aids, provide readings and resources, or help create relationship matches. If the program isn't supported by administrators who can be responsive, participants will not make the program a priority.

Another challenge is that while facilitators can observe a classroom and a learning management system can record e-learning clicks and tests, mentoring programs exist outside the control of a program leader or administrator. Mentoring conversations are not observed by a third party, and how learners apply what they have learned from a mentoring conversation is typically done on the job, away from direct observation of a program administrator. This lack of transparency can sometimes seem daunting. Practitioners in the talent development industry are often far more comfortable with learning they can easily observe and measure in a classroom than the type of growth that comes from connections in mentoring conversations. While performance improvement as a result of mentoring is measurable, there are fewer examples of how to measure it than more traditional learning approaches.

However, a relationship-based learning process such as mentoring will likely create far more effective results across your organization than staying within the comfortable bounds of classroom training or e-learning. Encouraging mentoring relationships to form, and supporting those relationships with the ideas described in this book, will help create deep learning experience; the impact will be more influential and last longer than traditional approaches.

The foundational idea is that mentoring programs are different in many ways from classroom training or e-learning. The approach to developing an effective, sustainable program requires a different mindset and strategy. Leveraging a process that takes the unique aspects of mentoring into account will set your program up for lasting success.

## How Mentoring Is Different From Coaching

If you do a quick search on "coaching versus mentoring," you will uncover a wide spectrum of definitions. However, these definitions can be distilled to the idea that mentoring is broad, covering both professional and personal issues, while coaching is task-oriented and focused on specific performance gaps. On the other hand, some well-established organizations such as the International Coach Federation (ICF) define coaching as "partnering with clients in a thought-provoking and creative process that inspires them to maximize their personal and professional potential, which is particularly important in today's uncertain and complex environment." So if coaching is a relationship that helps build on personal and professional potential, what is mentoring? Everyone has an opinion about the right answer, and it's true that mentoring and coaching are closely related.

In every client engagement, I work with teams to define mentoring for their organization because I have a mantra: "Words are important; language matters." For our purposes, this book takes a broad view to mentoring programs, which makes it more applicable across a wide variety of purposes. The following list of terms outlines the definitions we will use going forward in this book:

- Mentor: A more experienced individual providing some amount of guidance and support to another individual.
- Learner: A less experienced individual seeking guidance, support, or knowledge from another individual; also referred to as a mentee or protégé.
- Participants: The collective members of a mentoring program, including mentors and learners.
- Mentoring: The relationship between at least one learner and at least one mentor.
- Mentoring Program: A variety of structured and managed mentoring relationships within an organization.
- Coaching: A skill set used to help a learner grow and develop. It usually involves active listening and asking guided questions to encourage the learner to come up with solutions to issues.

Your organization's definition of mentoring doesn't have to be static; the critical thing is developing a common vision, even if it's one that evolves over time. Defining mentoring is incredibly important for your mentoring program's success, and it starts with clarity of purpose and mentoring philosophy.

An effective, long-lasting mentoring program cannot be developed if everyone is coming from a different perspective. It is very challenging to collaborate on building an effective mentoring program if we haven't all agreed on what we believe mentoring actually is! Maybe your organization aligns with the idea that mentoring is "a more informal association focused on building a two-way, mutually beneficial relationship for long-term career movement" (ATD 2015). Or perhaps your company believes mentoring "is a mutual discovery process in which both mentor and mentee have something to bring to the relationship ('the give') and something to gain that broadens each of their perspectives ('the get')" (Zachary 2002). Whatever your approach, the most important first step is to define mentoring within your organization. If you can gain agreement among major stakeholders, you've already taken a big step toward making your mentoring program successful.

## Mentoring Relationships Are About Connection

Every mentoring program is unique because it exists within a singular organization composed of an audience with specific needs, pursuing results important to that organization at that point in time. From program to program the structure, formality, complexity, management, and experience will differ. Even the language—terms for the mentor and learner, for example—will shift from one instance to another. However, the powerful common thread through all mentoring programs is connection. Mentoring is about relationships, which are more important now in our professional lives than they have ever been.

# The AXLES Framework for Developing Mentoring Programs

One obstacle for many organizations in building an effective and sustainable mentoring program is the lack of a tried-and-true process. The models that do exist aren't tailored specifically to developing mentoring programs, even though they are so different from any other type of talent development solution. Familiar models, such as ADDIE, don't work well when applied to mentoring programs. ADDIE is often criticized as a "waterfall" methodology that is rigid and unforgiving when projects change.

### What Is ADDIE?

ADDIE is one of the most popular approaches to developing learning solutions. This framework has five stages:
- A = Analysis is understanding the needs of the learners, content needs and gaps, and contextual organization information.
- D = Design is creating outlines, briefs, and other forms of explaining the potential flow of learning activities.
- D = Development is crafting and developing the various materials needed for the learning event. These include e-learning modules, participant guides, job aids, and slides.
- I = Implementation is providing the learning solution to learners.
- E = Evaluation is measuring the effectiveness of the learning solution.

While all of the components of ADDIE are addressed in some way during the development of a formal mentoring program, more flexibility is needed in the approach. Even more important, while ADDIE is useful for creating event-based learning solutions, it does not address the unique needs of a sustained learning relationship like mentoring.

In 2012, it became clear to me that we needed a better process—one that was easy to follow, but specifically created for mentoring programs, capturing the challenges and benefits that mentoring brings to organizations. For the next three years, I drafted and refined my model in several iterations. The final result—the AXLES model—is the framework for this book (Figure I-1).

**Figure I-1. The AXLES Model**

The AXLES model for developing mentoring programs is the first framework entirely devoted to the unique challenges of a sustained learning process. It is composed of five individual components—align, experience, launch, effectiveness, and support—each addressing a critical aspect of a mentoring program. These five components need to be planned and designed before a program launch. In addition, they create a checklist of the parts you need to maintain over the life cycle of the program.

The first component, Align to a Purpose, helps define the intention of the program. During this phase, program designers ask critical questions that will help make the program successful, and establish strategic partners for the organization. Every component of the model has a concrete deliverable that propels us toward results. In the Align to a Purpose stage, you will create a purpose statement. Aligning the program to the organization's needs ensures that the program's purpose is documented and gives the program direction during design and launch.

The second component is Design the Experience, during which design decisions are made for the program. Key choices are covered in this step, including program structure, schedule, participant matching, and expectations. Once the look and feel of the program is determined, you'll create the program charter. Like most deliverables, the program charter is a living document that changes throughout the program's development and life cycle.

Launch the Program is the third component. Launching your program is not the end of the road, nor is it a stand-alone event. Implementing a mentoring program for the first time (or annually, as you will see) is an important milestone, and part of a cohesive experience for participants. Example launch agendas for the program are provided, as well as other tools to help design the program launch.

During the fourth component of the program, you will Evaluate Effectiveness. During this component, you'll plan different types of important measures. The focus is on writing a meaningful story of the program's success using data from your evaluation plan.

Support Participants, the final component, is a phase during which you consider what your mentors and learners need to have a successful experience. This phase is intended to help you design and develop resources, webinars, videos, or other performance support aids. The deliverable of this component is a participant playbook, which usually includes important resources and tools for participants to refer to throughout the mentoring relationship. Learners and mentors should be equipped with the resources they need to make an impact and experience real and lasting change.

The strength of the AXLES model is its simplicity and intuitiveness, but it also considers the challenges and results of mentoring programs. A significant portion of the design can happen iteratively, focusing on the minimum viable product. Individuals and teams can work on any and all of the components of the model concurrently, as long as the design for all five components is completed before the mentoring program begins.

This process includes all the necessary steps to create a meaningful mentoring program. Each chapter in this book details one of the five steps and how it helps focus the work of developing a mentoring program.

## Broken Programs

Many existing mentoring programs are poorly developed, thanks to everything from poor planning and lack of alignment to a gap in participant support or failure to plan for program maintenance. Ineffective programs waste the time of both mentors and learners, and ultimately drain organizational resources. In addition, it becomes more difficult to gain buy-in for new mentoring programs when so many have been ineffective in the past.

Fortunately, organizations are looking for a solution. The AXLES model works for both new mentoring programs and programs that need to be diagnosed and improved. Throughout this book you will find specific references to how to leverage the AXLES model to iterate and improve ineffectual mentoring programs.

## The Way Forward

If developed correctly, mentoring programs have the potential to be the most effective tool in your talent development kit. Regardless of whether you are just beginning your journey to build a mentoring program, have already started, or are even working to improve an existing program, utilizing the AXLES model will put you on the path toward success.

In this book, you will find several features that will help you as you begin developing your mentoring program:

- Diagrams and images provide visual representations of concepts.
- Case studies written by industry leaders share specific experiences and best practices for developing mentoring programs.
- Key insights pull out the 10 most important ideas from each chapter.
- Chapter exercises give you the chance to put these ideas into action— remember, application is the best teacher!

Most important, as you read the ideas covered in this book, ask yourself, "How does this work for me, my mentoring program, and my organization?" Keep an open mind, but also treat each idea as a piece of a larger puzzle. You won't be able to connect every piece right away, but as you continue working on the project, you'll see how that piece helps you get to the goal.

---

## Mentors and Mentoring: More Relevant Than Ever

Michael Lee Stallard, President, E Pluribus Partners

The world has become increasingly complex, and additional skills are required to succeed. At the same time, research has shown that fewer family members and friends are available to help individuals develop the social and resilience skills necessary to cope with life's inevitable ups and downs. Mentors help fill this gap. Companies that meet this need for connection will have a competitive advantage in attracting and retaining talent. When McCann Worldgroup surveyed 7,000 Millennials, it found that their number one value was connection, which means that mentoring is becoming more important than ever.

## Specific Skills Mentor

The first type of mentor I learned from is the specialist who helped me develop specific skills and stop doing counterproductive things. This type of skills-based mentor can identify blind spots that are holding you back.

Take, for example, public speaking. Twila Thompson from The Actors Institute in New York City helped show me that decades of working on Wall Street had taught me to turn off my emotions when I spoke publicly. I would need to turn my emotions back on to connect with an audience. Twila and her colleague Gifford Booth trained me to make eye contact with one audience member at a time, and stay with that person until I could tell we had connected before moving on. They taught me to speak with greater volume and emotional range. At first it felt very uncomfortable, but they assured me it was not overbearing and was more engaging for the listener. I never would have figured this out on my own.

## Situational Mentor

A second type of mentor helped me during a difficult time in life. In 2004, my wife, Katie, was diagnosed with advanced ovarian cancer a year after she was treated for breast cancer. Between the plan prescribed by the medical team and research I did on my own, I struggled to find out what medical treatments would cure her. I wondered how I could best help her and our daughters, who were 12 and 10 years old at the time. When I posted Katie's diagnosis in online forums for ovarian cancer, patients and survivors responded, sharing their stories. Helen Palmquist, from Libertyville, Illinois, was especially helpful. She had a diagnosis similar to Katie's and had survived for more than 15 years. Helen mentored me through her emails and phone calls over the course of Katie's treatment. Those supportive conversations helped me cope with my own stress, fear, and anxiety, so that I could be there for my wife and daughters.

## Tacit Skills Mentor

Sometimes my mentors are not even aware that I think of them as mentors and am observing how they model certain behaviors. For example, my wife has extraordinary social intelligence and social skills. While I enjoyed connecting one-on-one, I was never at ease casually connecting in a group. Watching Katie in social settings helped me understand how she asks questions and interacts with people in ways that connect without going too deep. Thanks to Katie, I've become much better at this.

# The Mentor You Never Meet

I would not limit the pool of possible mentors to someone you can email, meet, or Skype with at an agreed-upon time. My own list includes several authors who have effectively mentored me through their books, which have inspired or challenged me. For example, Parker Palmer's *Let Your Life Speak: Finding the Voice of Vocation* helped me find the courage to change careers and start a new business. I've also learned a great deal about mentoring from Don Yeager, a former *Sports Illustrated* writer and editor turned corporate speaker. Don co-authored a fantastic book on the subject with the legendary UCLA basketball coach John Wooden (a.k.a. the Wizard of Westwood), titled *A Game Plan for Life*. Here are three pointers from that book:

## 1. Just Ask

Don't hesitate to ask someone to mentor you. You'd be surprised at how infrequently people ask others to be their mentor. In the book, Don recalls asking Coach Wooden to mentor him, assuming it was highly unlikely that he would. Coach Wooden said yes, and ended up mentoring Don for more than 12 years.

## 2. Failing to Prepare Is Preparing to Fail

Coach Wooden was known for focusing on preparation. He told Don that his job as a learner would require him to prepare a list of things he wanted to learn. As a result, Don spent two to three days preparing for each meeting with Coach Wooden. If you're asking someone to mentor you, be sure to spend sufficient time preparing in advance and developing an agenda for what you would like to learn.

## 3. For a Season

We tend to equate a mentoring relationship with a lengthy time commitment, which may preclude us from entering into one. However, what you need from a mentor may only require a single meeting or a few meetings. You may find that more people are open to the arrangement of being a seasonal mentor, sharing their wisdom on a particular area for a relatively short period of time.

---

### Key Insights: Introduction

1. Mentoring relationships are highly impactful and often more consistently effective than other types of talent development.
2. The number of poorly developed mentoring programs has created opponents to formal mentoring programs.
3. Unlike other types of talent development, until now there hasn't been a well-known, vetted process for developing a mentoring program.
4. The results of formal mentoring programs come from learning that happens outside the sphere of influence of program administrators.
5. Mentoring programs have the potential to bring about great results, but for them to be successful some unique challenges must be addressed.
6. The terms *coaching* and *mentoring* have many definitions. It's important to come up with a unique definition for your organization.
7. "Words are important; language matters."
8. Determine the purpose of your mentoring relationships and programs before you set out to design them.
9. Use the AXLES model to create a new mentoring program or improve an existing program.
10. Keep an open mind, and apply the ideas in this book to your specific situation.

## Chapter Exercises

### Individual Reflection Questions

Think about your experiences in mentoring relationships as a learner or mentor. (If you have never participated in a formal program as a learner or mentor, ask these questions of your supervisor or a colleague.)

- Describe a negative experience with a formal mentoring program. What made the experience negative?
- Describe a positive experience with a formal mentoring program. What made it positive?
- How do you define mentoring?

### Team Exercise

If you are currently working with a team to develop a mentoring program for your organization, or improving an existing program, answer the following questions collaboratively:

- What is our organization's working definition of mentoring? If we don't have one, who can help us create one?

- Who in our organization is going to be a champion for our program? How can we get them involved?
- Who might resist the program in our organization? Why? What can we do to alleviate their concerns?
- Discuss the AXLES model as a strategic plan for creating your mentoring program. How can we align this with our team's operating rhythm?

# STORIES OF EXPERIENCE

> When I'm preparing for a swim, I imagine absolutely every-
> thing about it: the color of the water, how cold it is, the taste
> of salt in my mouth. I visualize each and every stroke.
> —Lewis Gordon Pugh

## Mentoring Programs Come in All Shapes and Sizes

I have never seen two mentoring programs that are exactly alike. Even when they have many identical features, subtle differences in areas such as organizational culture play an important role in how participants experience the program.

Imagine that mentoring programs are like species of fish. They all have scales and fins and live in the water, but their colors, behaviors, food sources, and environments vary widely. Similarly, all mentoring programs are about connection, but the purpose, design, and outcomes are very different.

A common obstacle is that the people who are building the program have different ideas of what mentoring should look like—they may even use the same terms but mean different things. This is why talking about the mentor and learner experience is key in defining the outcomes of a mentoring program. By describing how the program is carried out, what it looks like, what learners are expected to do as a part of the program, and how mentors will be supported, we can begin to build a common understanding.

This chapter features five stories that illustrate different mentoring program experiences. Each anecdote is a patchwork of a real program and the learners and mentors who participated in it; these stories are true to the spirit of the many individuals I have had the pleasure of working with while preparing to write this book.

## Trey: A Learner in an Effective Informal Mentoring Program

"Life-changing." That's how I would sum up my mentoring experience. When they launched the program, I was one of the first to sign up and request a mentor. As a manager, I'm always looking for ways to be a better leader. At our organization we have a strong culture of learning from one another, so the mentoring program simply put more structure to what was already happening. The program administrators did a great job of communicating the purpose of the program, how it would work, and what we could expect if we participated.

The program was scheduled to run annually between February and October, and anyone who wanted to participate could register. All I had to do was give the program administrators some information about what I was looking for, and they provided a list of available mentors, their bios, and other relevant information. It was easy to find a potential mentor; the one I chose happened to be in my same role in another region. It turned out that other people in our roles across the company were also looking for a mentor, so we formed a six-person peer-mentoring group. It was perfect; we were already used to the group dynamic because of how collaboration-driven our organization is.

As a peer-mentoring group, we had access to sample agendas, tips on how to function in the group, and ideas about how to drive ourselves individually within the group. We had all the tools we needed to be successful. And it didn't end there. The program administrators reached out periodically to make sure we had everything we needed. We also received pulse surveys throughout our time together to give our feedback. A few people left over the course of the year, but a couple new folks joined us. The group is still meeting monthly with ad hoc calls as needed.

I have grown so much as a result of my peer-mentoring group. I set out to use mentoring as a way to become a better leader, and I can see the results. This program provided exactly what I needed to grow my skills, and I've been able to help others as well.

The programs that experience the best results are those that align their structure and design with the organization's culture. Some organizations thrive with informal, collaborative, or matrixed designs, while others expect a more formal structure. It is critical to take the time to understand what the organization's most important needs are and how to meet those needs with mentoring. These key factors will be discussed further in chapter 2, "Align to a Purpose."

## Rita: A Learner in an Effective Formal Mentoring Program

My experience in the mentoring program was great! The entire process was communicated well, and I knew what to expect along the way. As soon as I was accepted into the program, I received materials outlining what the program would consist of, meetings that would happen, and due dates. The program administrators explained that each learner would be matched with a mentor, and that the formal relationship would last for six months.

The program had a lot of moving pieces and was a good amount of work, but it was completely worth it. I completed an assessment, and was matched with a department head based on that and my individual development plan (IDP) goals. After the virtual launch event, we were expected to meet with our mentors at least every two weeks, and complete some assignments between meetings. It was a challenge to get it all done, but I knew what to expect because everything had been explained at the beginning of the program.

The program's structure worked great for us. My mentor and I had a game plan to work with, were never confused about what we should be doing, and knew where to get answers if we had questions. By the time my formal mentorship ended, I felt as though my IDP performance goals had improved a lot.

The learner and mentor experience is paramount for success in any mentoring program. This organization required a formal structure for the mentoring relationship, and the culture valued the extra effort spent in pursuit of talent development. Many organizations worry that learners and mentors are too busy to take on the demands of the mentoring relationship, but in reality many participants see the value and are more than willing to make the effort. Chapter 3, "Design the Experience," provides a step-by-step process for making design decisions about structure, schedule, and matching.

## Nathan: A Mentor in a Poorly Managed Mentoring Program

When HR asked me to be a mentor in the newly redesigned mentor-led group-mentoring program, I was happy to participate. They weren't looking for too much effort; just mentor a group of fewer than 10 people once a month. I learned later that the program is ongoing, with no planned end date. I've got plenty on my plate already, but as a senior leader in my organization, I know how important it is to develop our talent. So I agreed.

I have to say it was pretty disorganized. First they told me I would be working with a group on business acumen, which is right in my wheelhouse, so that was fine. But the week of our first meeting, they switched me to a group working on presentation skills. Hardly my strength! I'm not terrible at it, but I had no idea how to mentor a group of people on that topic. Then I had to scramble to do some research because the program administrators didn't have any resources to help me.

Our mentoring group "launch" was more like a false start. We didn't have an agenda for our meetings (until I made one) or an idea of how to set goals for the group. In addition, because I was given a group with a full 10 people, I'm sure some of them didn't get what they needed. I don't think anyone can be truly effective with that many people in the room. That first meeting was awkward and kind of disheartening.

Eventually, we got into a rhythm with our meetings, but not until after we had lost a few people. They just stopped showing up to meetings. I emailed the program administrator to let him know, but he had already heard and just hadn't communicated with me.

Overall, it was like that nightmare when you show up at school and realize you're naked. I was standing in front of 10 people with no idea of what to do. Instead of an inspirational start to our mentoring relationship, it was a terrible experience! I won't be signing up to mentor again after this.

A mentoring program's launch should be well thought out. Each connection point presents the possibility for the program to succeed or fail. Whether there is a large launch event, or a soft launch where mentoring relationships are formed, the beginning of the process is a critical time when expectations are met or not. For more information about ways to launch a mentoring program, refer to chapter 4, "Launch the Program."

## Indira: A Mentor in a Well-Managed Mentoring Program

As an organization, we have been looking for ways to increase our retention. The mentoring program is part of the solution we've been putting in place for the last year and a half. As part of the leadership team, I received updates about the mentoring program from the design team during the entire development process. They kept us informed of what they were trying to accomplish and how the program was being built to address the organization's most critical talent needs. Communication is really important to me.

When it came time to recruit mentors, I was all in. I had already seen how the program aligned with our strategic goals, so I knew how my participation would help us achieve results. Once we signed up, the program staff communicated thoroughly and often about expectations and milestones. They explained that each mentor would be assigned one learner, and that the formal relationships would be scheduled to last a full year. They even built in a six-month checkpoint when we could change learners if needed.

One aspect that really impressed me was the brief pulse surveys that the program administrators sent out to learners and mentors every two months to assess progress and gather feedback. They then shared the results of each survey and let us know how the feedback was influencing ongoing program improvement.

The program administrators also conducted focus groups periodically with a few participants to receive anecdotal feedback and get suggestions that might not be captured by a survey. Overall, they were focused on getting real impact data, and they did it in a way that didn't take too much effort from us. We weren't overloaded with long surveys that didn't get analyzed.

At the end of the mentoring relationship, both the learner and the mentor met with the learner's supervisor to discuss development and progress on the learner's goals. The results of those conversations were captured in our learning management system and given to the team.

I also completed a final survey about my assigned learner and her progress, as well as a final feedback survey about the program. My learner completed an evaluation of me as a mentor, which gave me some great insights on how well I performed my role as mentor.

Within two weeks of submitting our information, we received final reports of how we did compared with others in the program, as well as key insights to think about moving forward. The program team also continues to give the leadership team regular updates on several different factors. We receive quarterly status reports with data on mentoring relationships, learner goals, mentor scores, and so forth. We also get updates twice a year about how well participants in the program are doing back on the job with their new skills.

The best part, though, is our retention scores. Since we started the program 18 months ago, our retention numbers have started to move in the right direction. The program team has been able to show the program's success and its impact on retention. Our organization is seeing exactly what we hoped for thanks to the team's ongoing diligence in evaluating the program.

Evaluating mentoring programs can seem daunting. After all, we don't always do a great job of measuring the impact of training classes that happen within our span of control—how can we be responsible for mentoring that happens outside our reach? There are many ways to build an evaluation plan for mentoring programs to show results, gather feedback for the purposes of program improvement, and collect information on both mentors and learners. Chapter 5, "Evaluate Effectiveness," looks at the many options available for effectively measuring program success.

# Rachel: A Learner in an Ineffective Informal Mentoring Program

Every year, my company nominates two people from each department to be in the leadership development program. I've been looking forward to the opportunity for three years. After all, this training program is only available to a few people, and it includes a senior leader as a mentor. I couldn't wait!

Unfortunately, the reality turned out to be very disappointing. I didn't get any information before the program started, just a calendar invite to come to the training room on the date the program launched. I had no idea what to expect.

Don't get me wrong, I was still excited to get a mentor, but I was apprehensive about what I was walking into. I thought for sure this was a meeting where I would get to meet my senior leader mentor, maybe a vice president or director, and we could get started. Instead, the mentors weren't even at the meeting. The meeting was for the learners to fill out applications to be matched with mentors.

Fast forward to when I was finally matched with a mentor, who was a VP from another department that I respect a lot. You'd think the rest would be a slam dunk, but it was pretty awkward. For one thing, neither of us was sure why we were matched (not that I'm complaining!). Once we started our meetings, we weren't sure how to get started or what we should cover. We had to sort of feel out the relationship—I assumed she would know what our goals were or what we should discuss, but she said she was leaving it up to me. While it was nice spending time with her, some of our meetings were just social coffee and didn't really help me in the long run.

After a few months we got an email from the program administrator. (The only one after the program launched, by the way!) The email said that the program was ending for the current year and we should conclude our formal relationships. Well, you can imagine that if we didn't know how to start, we surely didn't know how to finish either!

Overall, I'm not really sure what I expected from the mentoring program, but it wasn't this.

Very often, mentoring programs fail, not because of design, but because of communication and alignment. Mentoring relationships get started and thrive in isolation from a facilitator or program manager, and need a strong foundation on which to build. Learners and mentors (even experienced ones) need clarity on what to expect from the program, how to best conduct their roles, and how to gauge success. Participant support is a theme throughout the book, but chapter 6, "Support Participants," goes deeper into the topic.

# Conclusion

Once on the path to developing a mentoring program, there are many options available to create a sustainable, impactful mentoring experience. The stories in this chapter are intended to help you think through the experience your participants should have, and influence your development process and design decisions.

Seeing the many factors that contribute to the success (or failure) of mentoring programs helps to illustrate why each step of the AXLES model is critical for developing mentoring programs. Each of the following chapters is aligned to a step in the AXLES model, and guides you through the process of aligning, designing, launching, evaluating, and supporting your unique mentoring program experience.

## Key Insights: Stories of Experience

1. Mentoring programs take many different forms.
2. Even within a development team, individuals have different visions of what a program should look like and what different terms mean.
3. Programs often fail due to lack of communication with participants, especially when learners and mentors do not feel supported.
4. Setting expectations for participant roles and effort is critical to a positive program experience.
5. Each organization's needs are unique, and taking time to align the mentoring program with strategic goals is the only way to see long-term results.
6. Mentoring programs succeed or fail based on participant experience throughout the program life cycle.
7. Mentors are linchpins when it comes to mentoring programs—supporting them and communicating with them is very important.
8. Program launches (no matter what form they take) are important to setting the stage for success in mentoring relationships.
9. Communicating with leadership during program development is a great way to generate interest and recruit mentors.
10. Evaluating the effectiveness of mentoring programs through multiple methods will help tell the story of the program's success.

# Chapter Exercises

## Program Visioning Activity

Consider the experience your learners and mentors will have in your program. Use the following questions to describe the program you are developing or adapting:

- What words or phrases do you want your learners to use to describe their experience in the program?
- What attributes of their experience in the program will be most important to your learners (mentor title, networking possibility, time and effort spent, measurable progress, and so forth)?
- What words or phrases do you want your mentors to use to describe their experience in the program?
- What attributes of their experience in the program will be most important to your learners (learner role, time and effort spent, measurable results, and so on)?

## Team and Stakeholder Exercise

If you are currently working with a team to develop a mentoring program for your organization, or improving an existing program, review your answers to the previous questions together. Then interview your key stakeholders, including the project sponsor, using the questions above.

# 2
# ALIGN TO A PURPOSE

*The object of all work is production or accomplishment and to either of these ends there must be forethought, system, planning, intelligence, and honest purpose, as well as perspiration. Seeming to do is not doing.*
—Thomas Edison

## Why Mentoring Programs Fail

Mentoring programs are not a new concept, even if mentoring program facilitators still seem unclear as to how to design and execute them systemically. Unfortunately the many failed, flavor-of-the-month formal mentoring programs have done a lot to hurt the effectiveness of one of the most powerful tools of talent development.

But how has this happened? Here's a typical example: Organizations seek nonclassroom training solutions to save time, money, or effort. They decide to implement a mentoring program because they believe it will be a simple design project. As a result, they don't spend the time and effort needed to execute the program correctly. These programs then run into an endless string of obstacles and ultimately fail publicly. They encounter issues such as poor participant experience, lack of support for mentors, or an inability to connect results with talent issues. Many organizations try again, but don't attempt to do anything fundamentally different, so they fail again.

Programs usually fail for one (or more) of three reasons:
- lack of alignment to the organization's top talent needs
- lack of planning for program scalability and sustainability
- lack of sponsor or stakeholder involvement and championship.

Each of these issues needs to be addressed before the design work begins. However, the alignment work needed to ensure success for mentoring programs is too often skipped. Why? There are many possible reasons. Perhaps the internal practitioners feel confident in their knowledge of the organization and culture, so they don't take time to do the critical foundational work. Or because senior leaders want immediate results, corners are cut to deliver fast. Maybe the project sponsor, who is usually the senior leader with the most influence on the project, has declared the need for a mentoring program, and the project team is concerned that any other alignment or analysis will offend or irritate her. No matter the reason, failure is inevitable.

If you are reading this book because you want to fix your mentoring program, take special interest in this chapter. Most likely, the ultimate reason for your program's demise lies in the alignment work discussed here. It is always worth spending the time to make sure everyone has the same vision for success before moving forward. If a program is intended to be long-lasting and fizzles out after six months, that constitutes failure. Likewise, if a program is well liked by participants, yet doesn't succeed in changing behavior and growing talent, it is still a failure.

The goal should be to start aligning the mentoring program to the organization, create a plan for scaling and sustaining the program, and take the time to get your sponsor and stakeholders involved from the beginning.

## Envisioning the End Product

To build mentoring programs that endure through the natural talent cycles of your organization, as well as programs that create real growth in your talent population, you need to begin with the end in mind.

First, those leading the design and implementation of a mentoring program (or a redesign) should have access to decision makers and the project sponsor. If you have been charged with the development of a program, but are getting your information from the sponsor or leadership secondhand, it's time to make a change. Create a situation in which you (the project lead) or your team has regular and ongoing access to the project sponsor, and ideally other stakeholders, too. To gain access, consider what you can do within the politics of your organization. Maybe you can ask your direct supervisor to include you in meetings with the project sponsor. Or, you could send an email status update to the sponsor with a note saying, "This would be a great opportunity for us to discuss the project face-to-face. Please let me know when you are available." Often, access is an issue because we either have not asked or haven't explained why access is critical to project success. Taking this step will help you establish long-term success.

After developing a partnership with stakeholders, continue by identifying those talent needs for the organization that are critical to success. I tell my clients, "We want to build a program that solves your most critical talent issue—not your second or third." While mentoring programs can be comprehensive enough to address multiple goals, keeping the main focus on the most critical talent need is key.

Once the focus has been identified, the mentoring program should be framed as the solution that will help resolve those issues. Mentoring could also be part of the solution—mentoring programs work tremendously well in cooperation with training programs and other talent solutions.

Now, let's dive into each step a little further. The following sections explain how to promote a positive consultative partnership, define mentoring for your organization, align to your organizational culture, understand talent needs and the business case for mentoring, describe the benefits of mentoring to mentors and learners, and define success.

## Promote a Positive Consultative Partnership

According to the Project Management Institute (PMI 2014), "An actively engaged sponsor is the top driver of project success." In their research, PMI has repeatedly found this to be true across project types and industries. The idea is especially relevant for a talent development solution like mentoring programs.

Our project sponsors, senior leaders, and stakeholders should be connected to the mentoring program development and become champions for the project. In short, they need to care. However, leaders have a lot on their plate and are often overextended, with many things fighting for their attention. To get noticed, you have to show them why they should care and that you can be a good business partner.

It is not enough to be competent and skilled as a talent development professional; you also must be an excellent consultative partner within your organization. Being the best partner means being able to identify those talent issues that keep senior leaders up at night and propose solutions to them. Mentoring programs are often a great solution because, when developed correctly, they can be adapted to address many of our most pressing talent issues. And because mentoring program results are built on sustained learning processes, they have the potential to deliver big results.

Practitioners often struggle to get access to senior leaders. Sometimes, it's related to politics; other times, someone's manager doesn't want to be bypassed or there is a culture of "that's the way we've always done it." While there's no surefire way to overcome this issue, it's important to challenge it. Sometimes, explaining the benefits of direct access will make a difference. You could also provide regular status updates, copying a manager to keep her in the loop.

It's important to encourage practitioners to find common goals that help bridge the gap. For example, explain that everyone involved with the project wants to see it succeed, and you believe that having regular meetings with the project sponsor is the key to that success. Once there is access, it is possible to demonstrate a positive consultative partnership.

As business partners, it is important to use language that resonates with leadership, rather than jargon specific to the talent development industry or human resources. Communicating with leaders in the way that they understand will give your ideas and suggestions the best chance for adoption; create connection through common language and understanding. Nancy Duarte (2010) says in her book *Resonate* that "connection is why average ideas sometimes get traction and brilliant ideas die—it all comes down to how the ideas are presented."

Listen to the language that is important to your project sponsors and senior leaders. Are they talking about the talent pipeline, retention, or value proposition? Are you using those terms as well? Are they referencing data and speaking about analytics? If so, make sure you are too.

When you show that you are listening and focused on the same things, senior leaders and project sponsors will see your value as a business partner.

## Define Mentoring for Your Organization

Take a moment to email 10 of your colleagues and ask them to define mentoring. You will probably get 10 different responses. Each will be correct to that person, and some may even contradict each other.

Mentoring is considered to be a method for a more experienced individual to develop a less experienced individual with specific, known performance gaps. However, this is a narrow definition and doesn't include the possibility of alternative mentoring relationships like peer or group mentoring. Your organization should develop its own definition or philosophy for mentoring before beginning to develop a mentoring program. Developing a mentoring program before there is agreement on what mentoring means to the organization is like building a house without a foundation.

This is even more applicable if you are beginning a program redesign. Most programs that have failed and need to be revived are in that position because the project team didn't define mentoring as it related to its organization. Take some time to do this with your project sponsor and stakeholders. Gaining a consensus would be ideal, so that development on the program can begin. However, if total agreement can't be reached, create a working draft to revisit throughout the process.

Here are some examples of mentoring definitions:

- "Mentoring programs provide employees the opportunity to learn from experts to develop and grow into who they want to become. Formal mentoring in organizations demonstrates a commitment to the employees, their professional development, and their success in the organization" (Way and Kaye 2011).

- "Mentoring: A more informal association focused on building a two-way, mutually beneficial relationship for long-term career movement" (Reitman and Benatti 2014b).
- "At ExperiencePoint, our mission is to 'make experience a better teacher by making it faster, safer and sharply focused.' As we continue to grow to meet our client needs, it's critical that every team member has access to impactful developmental opportunities to hone their skills and grow into their full potential. Mentoring relationships create the best environment for experiential, challenging and results-oriented growth for every team member" (ExperiencePoint).
- "The voluntary developmental relationship that exists between a person of greater experience and a person of lesser experience that is characterized by mutual trust and respect" (Army Field Manual; Harvey, Schoomaker, and Preston 2005).

No matter where you are in the design or redesign process, define your program first and encourage open dialogue. Ultimately, the clearer the group is on how your organization defines mentoring, the easier it will be to develop the mentoring program in later steps of the model.

## Tie the Program to Your Organization's Culture

A large part of the work in defining mentoring for your organization is understanding the culture and how it will influence the needs for mentoring. For example, if you are working with an organization that prides itself on organic learning relationships, that idea should be supported within the mentoring definition, and ultimately influence the design of the program. I once worked with an organization that has two core values: Develop Yourself and Others and Create a Legacy. So we used the same language for their definition and purpose statement, as well as all program documentation. There is more information about examining the influence of culture on the design of the mentoring program in chapter 3.

Keep an eye out for those items that are cultural signals, such as the mission, vision, and values statements; leadership development program models; recruiting or internal value propositions; and onboarding content. These documents are usually crafted with care to capture the essence of the organization's culture, and are the perfect indicator for how to proceed with the mentoring program definition and purpose statement.

# Understand Talent Needs and Business Case

To be as effective as possible in any talent development role, it's critical to understand the business and act in its best interests. Knowing how and when to be a consultative partner is one skill that helps with this. A consultative partner is a practitioner who aligns to the strategic needs of the organization, frames solutions in a way that addresses business issues, and is actively curious. This person is also usually able to challenge assumptions in a positive way by asking questions without disrupting the political landscape.

The benefit of being a consultative partner is that you are privy to the most critical needs of the organization. Most organizations face several challenges in talent development. Issues vary, but some of the most common include:

- attrition of top talent
- ineffective recruiting and onboarding
- long time to success in critical roles
- lack of leadership talent pipeline
- loss of institutional knowledge
- disengaged employees
- diversity and inclusion gaps
- job performance and skills gaps
- limited internal networks.

An organization might look at this list and check off many of the issues; it might even add a couple additional ones. However, you can usually focus on the most critical talent issue facing the organization—the issue that, if not addressed, will result in disaster. Because many of the most common talent development issues are interdependent—for example, onboarding and time to success or diversity and employee engagement—it might be possible to narrow the list down to the top two or three issues, if you can't decide on one overarching problem.

At this stage the goal is to recognize the most critical talent needs of the organization as viewed from the senior leadership perspective. A mentorship program built to address the most important talent needs of the organization is much more likely to continue to receive funding and support from the senior level than one focused on a less urgent issue.

The more public leaders are in their support of the mentoring program, the more likely the rest of the organization will follow suit and the program will gain in popularity. It will also be seen as more credible if senior leadership endorses it.

Another reason to focus on the most critical talent needs is to set the program up for success. If an organization's senior leaders are concerned about a specific talent issue, they will have thought about how to address it. On the other hand, if the program addresses a less urgent talent need, they probably have not given much thought about how to measure success. The issues that keep senior leaders and project sponsors up at night are the ones that already have goals attached to them. Finally, developing a sustainable and effective program is a significant investment of resources, so you need to make sure those resources are applied to the issues that will provide the best return.

After identifying the organization's most critical needs, the next step is relatively easy. Simply flip the negative issue to a positive by explaining how the mentoring program will be designed to achieve results. Use the phrase "As a result of our mentoring program, we will" to help create the business case for the program. Table 2-1 provides a few examples.

### Table 2-1. Mentoring Program Business Case

| Organizational Issue | As a Result of Our Mentoring Program, We Will |
|---|---|
| Attrition of top talent | Retain top talent |
| Ineffective onboarding | Effectively onboard new talent |
| Long time to success in critical roles | Decrease learning curve in critical roles |
| Lack of leadership pipeline | Build a substantial leadership pipeline |
| Disengaged employees | Increase employee engagement |
| Job performance and skill gaps | Grow job performance and close skills gaps |
| Limited internal networks | Build networking and sponsorship |

The idea behind this flipped approach is to state clearly, in business language, the purpose and intent of the mentoring program. This is the first step in gaining consensus. If the project sponsor, stakeholders, and project team agree with the purpose of the mentoring program, everyone is moving toward the same vision of success.

## Benefits to Learners and Mentors

As you continue through alignment work, you want to be sure to articulate how participants will benefit as a result of their time in the program. Organizations often begin developing a mentoring program because they have specific learner benefits or outcomes in mind, and it isn't uncommon for programs to list the benefits to learners. However, it's also important to tell mentors how participating in the mentoring program will benefit them as well. Mentors are the linchpin in a formal program. No matter how well designed it is, if your mentors aren't happy the program will not succeed. Table 2-2 lists the benefits to learners and mentors; some items are benefits for both groups, while others only benefit one.

## Table 2-2. Learner and Mentor Benefits

| Learner Benefits | Mentor Benefits |
|---|---|
| Greater understanding of organization's structure and business | Unique insight into the business |
| Professional development in key job areas | Leadership development |
| Unique opportunity for individualized feedback | Unique opportunity for individualized feedback |
| Broader, more strategic perspective | Broader, deeper perspective |
| Increased internal networks | Increased internal networks |

Taking the time and effort to articulate the benefits to the learners and mentors in your potential program will help influence design decisions and success factors when evaluating effectiveness.

## Define Success

In the talent development world, evaluating success is often (and unfortunately) an afterthought. After the foundational alignment and design work has been done, and the project has launched, the project team usually comes together to determine what metrics can be measured post-launch to indicate success. This way of measuring success is not only ineffective, but also very challenging and inefficient. Beginning to plan and measure effectiveness and impact after the program has launched is like trying to board a plane after it's already taken off. By the time the program is under way, it's much too late to figure out what success looks like.

Instead, it's important to define success from the first step in developing your mentoring program. After the program's purpose has been identified, the next step is to make that purpose measurable. When the success measures are defined first, the design can be shaped by how impact will be measured.

Many critical talent issues can be quantified with data. If the purpose of the program is to increase employee engagement, you might be able to use existing assessments and processes to set goals and measure success. Successful recruitment and talent onboarding is also usually easy to attach to quantifiable measures. You can leverage these existing measures as the success factors of your mentoring program. During your ongoing meetings with the project sponsor, set aside time to talk about how success can be measured for the program's stated goal.

Keep in mind that many organizations' most critical talent needs are very complex. In chapter 5, "Evaluate Effectiveness," success is defined in terms of large, complicated goals, such as diversity and inclusion. While these may not be directly measureable, it's still important to track them to find out how they're affected by the mentoring program. One model that works well for measuring impact is the New World Kirkpatrick Model, which is explained further in chapter 5.

I've also worked with several organizations that preferred more qualitative measures of success. For example, one program's goal was to increase internal networks and cross-functional relationships. Success was reported through a series of anecdotes about high-potential talent who had expanded their networks and learned more about the different functions of the organization. In that situation, the subjective information of participant stories was exactly what that leadership team wanted to hear.

Before concluding your work in the Align to a Purpose step of the model, take the time to work with your project sponsor and stakeholders to define success as clearly as possible. While the actual measurement of the goal might shift during the project's life cycle, it is still very important to establish a common vision. This measure, whether quantitative or qualitative, acts as the main reference point as you continue developing or redesigning the mentoring program.

## Mentoring Program Purpose Statement

The tangible deliverable from the Align to a Purpose step is a mentoring program purpose statement (Figure 2-1). This serves as the first point of agreement among the project sponsor, stakeholders, and project team members. The benefit of this deliverable is that it is reusable and becomes a go-to resource throughout the project's life cycle. It essentially becomes an all-in-one default for how you describe the mentoring program.

The purpose statement is typically anywhere from a few sentences to a few paragraphs. It includes the:

- definition of mentoring for the organization
- cultural impact
- talent needs
- business case
- benefits of program to mentors and learners
- definition of program success.

## Figure 2-1. Example Purpose Statement

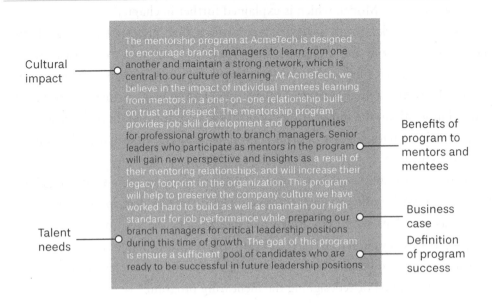

Cultural impact

The mentorship program at AcmeTech is designed to encourage branch managers to learn from one another and maintain a strong network, which is central to our culture of learning. At AcmeTech, we believe in the impact of individual mentees learning from mentors in a one-on-one relationship built on trust and respect. The mentorship program provides job skill development and opportunities for professional growth to branch managers. Senior leaders who participate as mentors in the program will gain new perspective and insights as a result of their mentoring relationships, and will increase their legacy footprint in the organization. This program will help to preserve the company culture we have worked hard to build as well as maintain our high standard for job performance while preparing our branch managers for critical leadership positions during this time of growth. The goal of this program is ensure a sufficient pool of candidates who are ready to be successful in future leadership positions.

Benefits of program to mentors and mentees

Business case

Talent needs

Definition of program success

# Mentor Program Alignment in a Mental Health Setting

Kelly Irons, Founder, developUs

Several years ago I was responsible for developing programming for several residential mental health treatment facilities in Philadelphia and the surrounding area. The programs served young women from the ages of 12 to 21 who had psychological disorders and had been removed from their caretakers for treatment purposes. The clinical staff provided therapeutic treatment, and the residential staff kept them safe and helped them grow up. The clinical staff functioned as therapists, and the residential staff functioned as mentors, with a common goal of teaching the young women the skills to grow into fully functioning, well-adjusted adults.

Sometimes they learned daily living skills (doing laundry, getting up on time for school, cooking healthy meals); other times the skills were less tangible but even more critical to long-term success (identifying triggers, naming emotions, developing coping skills). Either way, it was truly a skills-based mentoring program that was highly integrated with each girl's therapeutic treatment plan.

Because of the focus on mental health treatment, it was critical for the mentoring component to be rooted in psychology. As a result, we developed a five-stage mentoring program based on Erik Erikson's first five stages of development (Figure 2-2).

## Figure 2-2. Stages of Psychosocial Development

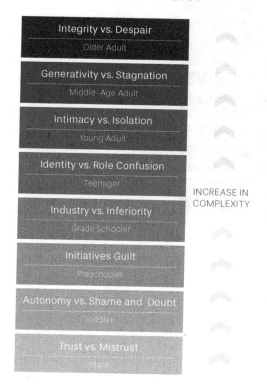

STAGES OF PSYCHOSOCIAL DEVELOPMENT

Integrity vs. Despair
Older Adult

Generativity vs. Stagnation
Middle-Age Adult

Intimacy vs. Isolation
Young Adult

Identity vs. Role Confusion
Teenager

INCREASE IN COMPLEXITY

Industry vs. Inferiority
Grade Schooler

Initiatives Guilt
Preschooler

Autonomy vs. Shame and Doubt
Toddler

Trust vs. Mistrust
Infant

Every resident in the program entered into the relationship with her assigned mentor at the first stage, which we called "Hope." The goals of the mentor–learner relationship at this point were to assess and resolve the Trust vs. Mistrust conflict represented by Erikson's model. In nonpsychological terms, this meant answering two fundamental questions for the residents of the program: "Am I safe here?" and "Can you help me?" From there, residents progressed through additional levels, each corresponding with the next stage in psychosocial development until they reached the fifth and final stage, which we called "Identity," the language of which we borrowed directly from Erikson's model (Figure 2-3).

Because the mentors rarely had a psychology background, and many had no college education at all, it was critical that we aligned our goals in a way that those who were actually doing the work could understand. The program was constructed so that the end goal for both the therapeutic staff and the residential staff was the same—everyone wanted the young women to be successful. Because the learners were able to actively participate in the development process, the entire therapeutic environment was reinforced and progress was made in measureable ways.

## Figure 2-3. Development Questions Adapted From Erikson Model

| | |
|---|---|
| **Trust vs. Mistrust: Hope** | Am I safe here? Can you help me? |
| **Autonomy vs. Shame and Doubt: Will** | What happens when I act out? What are the consequences for my behavior, good and bad? |
| **Initiative vs. Guilt: Purpose** | What am I trying to accomplish? What goals do I have? |
| **Industry vs. Inferiority: Competence** | What are my natural strengths and limitations? What skills do I need to develop? |
| **Identity vs. Role Confusion: Identity** | Who am I as a person? |

We taught the language of the program to the girls, and talked about it in treatment meetings. Their progress through these stages was measured by the mentor and correlated closely to the progress the clinical staff saw. Many of the program participants could self-identify their stage of development, and set goals for how to reach the next one. (They knew the goal was to get to the fifth stage, "Identity," at which point we would refer them to a more independent living program.) I'm thrilled to say that many of the participants of that program, both the staff and the young women, still keep in touch, even after more than a decade.

Today, when I work with corporations and schools to build mentoring programs, I apply many of the same elements. You have to clearly establish the purpose, or the "identity" so to speak. You also have to give people a clear way to measure and talk about the success. Everyone should always be aware of where they are on the journey, and the appropriate next steps to take to effectively move through the program toward the goal. Whether it's a mentoring program for at-risk youth or corporate leaders, the goals are still the same: Develop fully functioning and well-adjusted students, tradesmen, teachers, engineers, accountants, customer service reps, rocket scientists, and leaders.

# Conclusion

Align to a Purpose is the first step in the AXLES model, and it is arguably the most important: The discovery and foundational work done during this step sets up the entire program for success. Without it, the program is aimless, without purpose, and likely to fail.

I have seen too many programs fail because they did not align with the organizations' most pressing talent needs. I have witnessed programs that fizzle out because they were not set up to meet the needs of a growing company or were not designed with long-term sustainability in mind. And of course, too many fail to gain individual support and the involvement of the project sponsor and other senior leaders.

Make sure that you become a trusted business partner. Speak the language that resonates with senior leaders, and don't use talent development jargon. It's important to identify the organization's talent issues and explain to project sponsors why the program is worth their attention. You must also take the time to work with the project sponsor and senior leaders to create a working definition for mentoring that takes into account important cultural influences such as hierarchy, political climate, and physical location of participants. This definition will help motivate everyone involved to move in the same direction by agreeing to a common vision of mentoring, which will lead to a discussion about top talent needs. Addressing the talent issues that are most critical to the organization will help set the program up for success because leaders are more likely to continue to support (vocally and financially) a program focused on strategic needs. Then you can frame the business case for the mentoring program by stating how the program will address those talent needs.

The business case leads to a statement about program success: How will we know if the program is successful? If it helps move the needle on critical issues, such as retention, engagement, and talent pipeline, and also delivers on the business case, it's a success. It may or may not be possible to define specific measures of success at this stage, but refinement during the process is to be expected.

After the discovery and alignment work is finished, everything is combined in the mentoring program purpose statement. This relatively brief document is the foundation on which the rest of the design and development work relies upon. If the project sponsor and project team can create and agree to a purpose statement, the rest of the design will move forward smoothly because the most difficult conversations have already occurred.

Finally, keep in mind that there are situations in which the entire Align to a Purpose step can be hashed out during a one-hour collaborative meeting, and others in which it will take weeks to get to a working purpose statement. The factors that most influence time and effort are:

- how much you have demonstrated your value as a consultative partner and have access to the project sponsor
- how much experience you have in facilitating conversations similar to the ones needed for defining mentoring, identifying critical talent needs, and establishing a business case for mentoring.

The more experience you have as a valued, consultative business partner and in guiding collaborative discussions among leadership, the quicker this step will go. If either or both of these experiences are new, this stage may take a bit longer. However, this work is fundamentally critical to success. You will never regret taking the time to create alignment for your mentoring program to be successful.

### Key Insights: Align to a Purpose

1. Mentoring programs tend to fail because of a lack of alignment with talent needs, lack of planning for program sustainability, or a lack of sponsor involvement.
2. It is critical to gain regular and unhindered access to the project sponsor and project stakeholders.
3. Position yourself as a business partner by demonstrating a positive consultative skill set.
4. Use language that resonates with senior leaders and project sponsors to show that the mentoring program is being brought in as a key solution.
5. Work with project sponsors and other stakeholders to define mentoring for your organization so that you can create a common vision moving forward.
6. Be aware of the most important and critical talent needs of the organization. By addressing these issues, you will earn support from senior leaders.
7. Use positive language to reframe talent needs as the business case for mentoring.
8. Use the business case statement as a step to gain consensus from the group about the direction of the mentoring program.
9. Make the time to articulate the benefits of participation for both learners and mentors.
10. Use language that is resonant within your organization to define success for the mentoring program. This will make it easier to evaluate program effectiveness throughout the project life cycle.

## Chapter Exercises

### Alignment and Discovery Meetings

Use the following questions and prompts to facilitate a series of meetings with your project sponsor and project team. Consider including other key stakeholders throughout the process. This can be done in one longer meeting if that is easier to schedule. (See appendix A for additional clarification.)

- What did not work well about this program? What worked well and is important to keep in the next iteration? (For programs needing redesign.)

- What attributes of the organization's culture should be captured for the program? (Consider mission, vision, and values and other documents.)
- How should mentoring be defined for this organization? (Use descriptive phrases wherever possible.)
- What are the organization's most critical talent needs? (Limit to one primary and up to three secondary needs.)
- How can we make the business case for a mentoring program? What are the solutions (part or whole) that this mentoring program will bring to the organization?
- What benefits are possible for mentors and learners who participate in the program?
- What are the quantitative or qualitative measures of success for the mentoring program? (It is OK to draft measures at this point and come back to refine them in later steps.)

## Mentoring Program Purpose Statement

Using the responses to the questions above, craft a draft program purpose statement. The goal is to create a working document that the project team can agree on, and that will continue to evolve as needed during program development.

Remember your purpose statement might be a few sentences or a few paragraphs, and should include:

- the definition of mentoring for the organization
- the cultural impact
- talent needs
- the business case
- benefits to mentors and learners
- the definition of program success.

# 3

# Design the Experience

## Building the Mentoring Experience

During the design phase, things start to come together and you begin to see the tangible results of your hard work. You have determined the purpose and direction of your mentoring program; now it's time to get your hands dirty.

Most programs start their life cycle in the design phase without any up-front foundational alignment work. Those are the programs that either never quite get off the ground or fail shortly after they've been implemented. Building a mentoring program the right way, with all the alignment work already under your belt, helps to create a path forward that is smoother and more likely to be successful.

Designing and developing mentoring programs isn't always automatic, because unlike face-to-face or live virtual training, mentoring programs are based on experiences that occur "out there," not under the traditional control of the learning function. Part of the work when designing live and virtual learning is establishing the classroom. However, mentoring programs don't rely on classroom experiences; instead, they're about relationship-driven learning. The benefit is tremendous, and a well-designed mentoring program can create lasting and effective relationships.

If you haven't had many experiences participating in or creating mentoring programs, it may seem daunting to try to shape one from scratch. However, once you're armed with the right process and tools, you'll have everything you need to confidently move forward. This chapter highlights the path, provides support and guidance, and gives you plenty of examples.

These tools are especially critical for ineffective programs that require a minor facelift (or a total overhaul). You should spend a considerable amount of time thinking about how you would like the experience of your learners and mentors to be different from what you have or don't have now. This will help ensure that your program creates a better learning experience for your participants.

There are many factors to consider when you design your mentoring program. For the experience to take shape, you have to combine a set of five interlocking design decisions (Figure 3-1).

## Figure 3-1. The 5 Mentoring Program Design Decisions

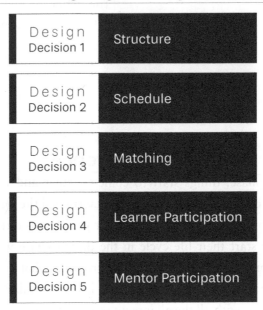

Each decision should be addressed in order. However, keep in mind that it's not necessarily a linear process—a choice you make later in the process may spark a slightly different decision in one of the earlier pieces. If you are working collaboratively on a team, this is especially true. It's normal for one design decision to influence another, or to go back to an earlier decision and adjust it based on newly discovered information.

Embrace the flexible nature of the design process. You want to provide participants with a valuable experience and return on investment to the organization. While it may seem easier in the short term to follow a linear process and be done, a more fluid design approach will usually provide better long-term results.

## Cultural Alignment

Before diving into the design process, keep in mind that your organization's culture will have a big influence on the decisions you need to make. For example, traditional and deeply hierarchical organizations tend to expect a more traditional approach to mentoring. On the other hand, organizations that are more innovation focused with shallow hierarchies and open work structures tend to favor more peer-led mentoring initiatives without much structure. No decision is objectively right or wrong; it just depends on the organization's culture.

This is why it is so important that you have a deep understanding of the culture, rather than simply being told about it. If you do not have firsthand experience about similar development initiatives, make sure you become acquainted with the culture by talking to people on the development team.

I once worked with an organization that prided itself on being "cutting edge" for its field. The organizational chart was relatively shallow, meaning that there were only five levels between the individual contributor and the very top. There were aspects of the company that were innovative, but it was fairly traditional at its roots. If I had taken the word of the project sponsor, the VP of professional development, at face value, the program I designed would have been a poor fit for the culture, and would not have provided the value we set out to achieve.

As you look at each of the design decisions in this chapter, consider them in light of your unique culture. How will a decision resonate with your senior leaders? What about your potential learner and mentor populations?

## Design Decision 1: Mentoring Program Structure

What does a mentoring program look like? One of the challenges of developing a mentoring program is that they come in all shapes and sizes. Some barely have structure; they're just a launch event followed by flexible expectations for the participants. Other organizations have deep, extensive programs led by internal champions with intricate participant matching and evaluation processes. All parts of the spectrum are valid, depending on the needs of the organization.

Four basic types of structures are commonly used for formal mentoring programs. In the business world, many programs are set up as hybrids to leverage the best qualities of each. Figure 3-2 provides an overview of each basic structure. Later in the chapter we'll combine the structures to demonstrate how to use their best aspects in a hybrid format.

The following pages present each type of program structure, as well as their risks and benefits. The most important point to remember is to keep the goal in mind. What did you set out to accomplish with this program? The purpose will help guide each decision you make during the design process.

## Figure 3-2. Program Structure Types

| Structure Type | Description |
| --- | --- |
| Traditional or One-on-One | A single learner is matched with a single mentor. The match is based on criteria aligned to program goals. The mentor acts as a guide, sponsor, and coach for the learner. |
| Reverse Mentoring | Younger employees act as mentors and are matched with older employee learners to address specific content topics, usually technology or diversity and inclusion. |
| Mentor-Led (Group Mentoring) | A single mentor is matched with a cohort of learners who are usually working on the same competency, skill, or goal. |
| Peer-Led (Mentoring Circles) | A group of individuals create a peer-mentoring community to work on specific skills or focus areas. |

# Structure A: Traditional or One-on-One

The traditional structure of a mentoring program is a relationship between one learner and one mentor (Figure 3-3). This is the most common because it tends to create the deepest and most influential relationships. Individual relationships allow the learners and mentors to build trust, which helps them dive deep into areas of strength and development. Mentors are often most familiar with this structure. Learners in this structure often feel empowered because of the individualized attention that a dedicated mentor acting as a coach and sponsor can provide. This structure also tends to work very well in more traditional organizations, which also tend to have an expectation that the one-one-one structure works best.

There are tremendous benefits to individual mentoring relationships. This structure is a significant investment in your talent, because these relationships tend to be authentic and long-lasting, and usually lead to significant and observable learner development progress. On the other hand, keep in mind that this structure also has its drawbacks. A one-on-one program requires a larger pool of mentors. I usually recommend trying to find more mentor candidates than learners, so that you can make sure there is ample opportunity for a good match. In addition, more relationships often mean that more is required from a logistics, tracking, and matching standpoint. (More on this later.)

The biggest risk with a traditional structure is access. By definition, your best mentors will be matched with only a few of the learners, which means that those learners have more access than others. Star-performing mentors will be in high demand, and some learners won't get to build the same kind of relationships with them.

## Figure 3-3. One-on-One Structure

Traditional or one-on-one mentoring is commonly used when:

- deep, authentic, and trusting relationships are the highest priority
- emphasizing relationships and interpersonal growth is important
- aligning with existing programs
- organizational culture is traditional or hierarchical in nature

- an organization's culture or leadership has the preconceived idea that traditional mentoring is best
- there is high resource availability, such as a mentor pool and a dedicated program administrator
- evaluating learner development and performance growth.

You should use avoid using it when:

- the organization is innovation-centered and nonhierarchical
- learners are proficient at networking and seeking informal mentors
- consistent messaging of content is the highest priority

- few mentors are available
- potential mentors are unskilled and will not help learner development
- staff cannot spend time administrating and supporting the program.

## Traditional Program Structure: Example 1

Lia has been identified as a high-potential branch manager at the financial institution where she works. She has been selected to be a part of a mentoring program and was matched with Sydney, the VP of operations for the Northeast United States.

- Benefits to Mentor: Sydney will get exposure to next generation talent, gain perspective on other regional operations, and enhance her skills in active listening, coaching, and leading through influence.
- Benefits to Learner: Lia will gain exposure to leadership and perspective from another region, learn key leadership skills from a respected member of the senior staff, and have an opportunity to network and gain insights into her career options.
- Benefits to Organization: The organization will see increased capability in key talent (Lia), increased engagement from senior leaders (Sydney), and a broader pipeline of talent for crucial leadership positions that are expected to open in the next few years.

## Traditional Program Structure: Example 2

At a custom parts manufacturer, a traditionally structured program has been put in place for all new hires to acclimate them to the organization's culture. On his first day as a welder with the company, Brandon was introduced to Jackson, a driver who had been with the company for 15 years, instead of being shown to the shop.

Jackson partnered with Brandon on all basic orientation tasks, and they continued to meet regularly for a year while Brandon transitioned into his role.

- Benefits to Mentor: Jackson has the opportunity to increase his legacy of leadership, enhance his skills, diversify his core responsibilities, and increase his network with other job functions and roles.
- Benefits to Learner: Brandon gains a sponsor and unofficial guide to the organization; he'll learn the culture's "unwritten rules," increase his understanding of the business, and gain influence in other parts of the company.
- Benefits to Organization: The organization maintains and strengthens its culture by having more experienced mentors guide new hires, which increases capability across the job functions.

## Structure B: Reverse Mentoring

Reverse mentoring is typically used when younger employees have a skill set (usually technology related) to teach older employees (Figure 3-4). It is the least common structure because of the assumptions involved. This format assumes that older employees need help with technology and younger employees are able to facilitate that development. Depending on your organization, this sounds like either a brilliant approach or an HR nightmare waiting to happen.

Reverse mentoring has been successfully applied in situations in which all participants feel an affinity for the idea and are excited for the learning opportunity, such as in smaller organizations with a tight-knit community. In contrast, larger organizations with geographically dispersed talent would have a much tougher time communicating this idea without offending someone.

In some organizations, the term *reverse mentoring* actually refers to roles or levels within the organization, rather than mentoring by age. For example, an individual contributor employee might mentor a senior manager–level employee. This is generally a more effective, and HR-safe, approach. Of course, the real benefit of this structure is that learning is expected in both directions. Employees will learn just as much from their exposure to leadership as leaders will learn by working with their employees.

While this structure can be very successful in the right situation, it's risky. It requires broad assumptions about groups of people (by age or role), and unless you have total buy-in from participants, you run the risk of offending people. Choose this structure only if it addresses your organization's specific talent needs.

## Figure 3-4. Reverse Mentoring Structure

Reverse mentoring is commonly used when:

- engaging individual contributor employees
- creating exposure between senior level leaders and those layers below
- some technological or other performance need is identified in the senior level population

- trying to attract Millennials to your organization
- there is high resource availability, such as a dedicated program administrator.

You should avoid using it when:

- considering age as a factor for determining relationship or need
- senior leaders are only participating for appearances, or have not fully bought in to the mentoring process
- there are not enough mentors—you need many more mentors than you would in a traditional style

- support cannot be provided to learners and mentors
- potential mentors are unskilled
- staff cannot spend time administrating and supporting the program.

## Reverse Mentor Structure Example

Nathan is an associate at a local chain of retail stores. He's been with the company for a year and is a top performer. Nathan is matched as a mentor to Christine, the manager of another store, to help her get a handle on the company's new social media campaign.

- Benefits to Mentor: Nathan has an opportunity to stretch his responsibility, gain perspective on other store operations, contribute to the company's overall strategic success, and enhance his mentoring and coaching skills.
- Benefits to Learner: Christine gains key skills needed to meet her goals in the social media campaign; she will also have an opportunity to work closely with one of the company's high-potential employees.
- Benefits to Organization: The organization benefits from Christine and other managers being better equipped to support the social media campaign, as well as higher engagement from mentors participating in the program and increased skill and capability in the manager learner population.

## Structure C: Mentor-Led

Mentor-led groups (also called group mentoring) are small groups of learners led by a single mentor who leads discussions about a common competency or skill set

(Figure 3-5). They are best represented by "brown bag lunch sessions" or "lunch-and-learns." Mentor-led groups work especially well when senior leaders and other mentors who are driven to mentor talent in their organizations but have little time to contribute to a full-scale mentoring program. The structure allows for greater impact across multiple people in the same amount of time.

Mentor-led groups also help spread out mentor resources if your mentor pool is small. By pairing a group of learners who are focused on similar goals or skills with a single mentor who excels in those areas, the learners can all benefit from a single source of development.

## Figure 3-5. Mentor-Led Group Structure

Mentor-led groups are commonly used when:

- fewer mentors are available
- creating exposure between senior-level leaders and those layers below
- emphasizing specific growth areas needed across a group of learners
- consistent messaging is important

- the organization's leadership has a strong desire to be a part of the process
- there is lower administration bandwidth
- combining with traditional or other structures for a holistic mentoring approach.

You should avoid using them when:

- leadership is unable to reliably make meetings and set time aside
- organization or leadership has preconceived ideas about mentoring programs

- mentors are not skilled in facilitating groups
- specific evaluation of performance or development growth is needed.

## Mentor-Led Group Structure Example

A group of six customer account executives are participating in a six-month mentor-led mentoring program. The group meets with their mentor from 2 to 4 p.m. on the first Thursday of each month. The marketing director, Lillian, mentors the group for the first three months in the area of industry knowledge. Then for the second half of the program, the group focuses on consultative selling with Scott, an account executive from a different business unit.

- Benefits to Mentors: Both Lillian and Scott have an opportunity to hone their skills in active listening, coaching, facilitating groups, and leading through influence. They also gain exposure into other areas of the organization.
- Benefits to Learner: The customer account executives gain critical skills.
- Benefits to Organization: The organization sees increased capability in key talent, as well as increased engagement from leaders like Lillian and Scott, while efficiently using the time of all involved.

## Structure D: Peer-Led

Peer-led mentoring groups (also called mentoring circles) are communities that get together to coach and guide one another, usually through a common topic or competency (Figure 3-6). These are groups of employees (regardless of role or title) who are committed to helping one another with self-development.

Because there is no assigned mentor, this structure does not bring established expertise into the mentoring relationship. It does, however, naturally build community within the group and empower group members. This has many long-lasting benefits for the organization.

Peer-led mentoring groups work well in flatter organizational structures, flexible work environments, and learning cultures in which peers are driven to help one another develop. This structure allows individuals to develop their leadership skills as they rotate through leading the group, which also provides tremendous value for the organization.

### Figure 3–6. Peer-Led Mentoring Structure

Peer-led mentoring is commonly used when:

- few mentors are available
- emphasizing community and employee engagement
- resources such as program administration are limited
- an urgent learning need has been identified, and groups of employees can help one another develop without needing an "expert."

You should avoid using it when:

- content is complicated and requires someone with experience to help facilitate
- the organization's culture is highly structured and compliance driven
- support is not available to help peer groups develop process and rapport
- specific evaluation of performance or development growth is needed.

## Peer-Led Structure Example

A group of five employees from across departments in an organization are matched for a peer-mentoring group focused on presenting skills. Individuals in the group were identified through their IDPs. After the initial invite, the group discusses tactics and tips over email.

- Benefits to Mentors: There are no formal mentors in this structure.
- Benefits to Learner: Learners have the opportunity to grow and develop in a specific area, gain community, and seek support from their peers. They also gain skills in developing others.
- Benefits to Organization: The organization increases capability and engagement in these groups.

# Hybrid Approaches

The goal in designing a mentoring program is to address known needs in the learner population using methods that are effective for organizational culture. Each of the basic mentoring structures has benefits and risks or costs—combining or hybridizing the structures helps to overcome the risks or costs of using each program alone.

To create a more holistic approach to mentoring relationships, you want to first think about your purpose statement and program goals. This will point you to a primary structure, which will serve as your starting place.

After choosing a primary structure, you can review each of the mentoring types and determine which ones to combine to create a unique program that either offsets the risks or costs of the primary structure or adds additional value. Figure 3-7 demonstrates an example of this process.

## Figure 3-7. Hybrid Example

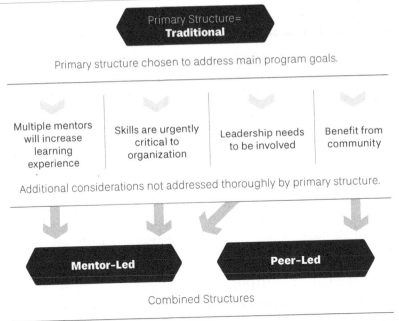

Combined structures give us the flexibility to address all our needs and constraints. They give shape to the experience of our learners and mentors, and provide a richer learning environment. Figures 3-8 and 3-9 are two examples of hybrid program structures.

## Figure 3-8. A Mentor-Led and One-on-One Hybrid

A mentoring program launches with a mentor-led session event. Several four-person groups are led by a mentor for a two-hour discussion on a specific skill or competency. At the end of the launch even, all learners are assigned a mentor for an ongoing traditional mentoring relationship.

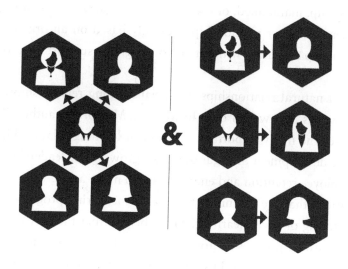

## Figure 3-9. A Mentor-Led and Peer Group Hybrid

A mentoring program is scheduled for one year, alternating mentor-led groups with peer groups each month. The group is focused on business acumen and time management, so two mentors who are experts in those areas take turns leading the group during the mentor-led sessions. Individuals in the peer group rotate responsibility for setting up their bimonthly meetings.

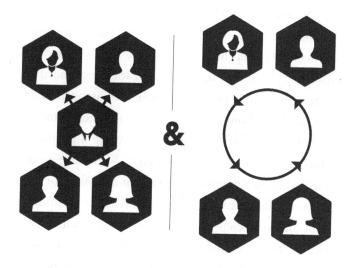

# What About Informal Mentoring?

Informal mentoring, which has many definitions, has become more prevalent in recent years. Most people refer to it as an unstructured relationship in which one or both parties are committed to learning from the other. These as-needed relationships are not set up, maintained, or tracked by the organization in any way. In other words, the mentor-learner relationship is usually based on an organic connection, and the relationship continues without any oversight or support by a formal mentoring program.

The idea of natural relationships, or social learning relationships, accelerating employee growth is a powerful one. In *Modern Mentoring*, author Randy Emelo (2015) discusses the many important ways social learning relationships can transform employee development at organizations—growing the leadership pipeline and increasing employee retention and engagement, to name a few.

Organizations that are beginning to develop mentoring programs often discuss informal mentoring or social learning. Many believe that the best way for mentors to help their learners grow is to form organic relationships without the help or structure from the organization. In some ways, this is absolutely true. Relationships that evolve organically can certainly last longer and create more impact than those introduced artificially.

## Bringing in Social Learning

There are many times when social learning is exactly what an organization needs, but it isn't quite ready to incorporate that style of mentoring. For example, social learning tends to be more of a challenge in organizations with cultures that are siloed, political, hierarchical, or traditional. In these organizations, would-be mentors and learners may need help navigating what it means to have an effective mentoring relationship. In addition, the organization may need to track the progress, goal attainment, or other evaluation measures associated with the program; this is nearly impossible without formal elements in place. Finally, if you do all the alignment work and other efforts that go into creating a purpose statement, you'll know whether your program has a defined goal. Without evaluation, it would be very difficult to tell what role mentoring played in attaining (or missing) that goal.

In organizations without a strong foundational learning culture, informal mentoring is inconsistent and very challenging to assess for results. With these organizations, you should institute a staged approach to build the mentoring and coaching capability within the organization, and then peel back the structure and administration as needed. Figure 3-10 shows how a traditional program might be scaled back over time to create a social learning culture.

## Figure 3-10. Moving From Traditional Mentoring to Social Learning

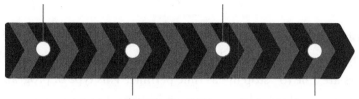

Launch ongoing formal mentoring program with traditional structure, administrative check points, learner and mentor support

After 12 months, remove formal learner and mentor support, provide on as-needed basis, communicate repository of support materials on intranet

Over 6 to 12 months, provide support, track questions, and continue to facilitate matching between mentors and learners

After 18 months, provide alternate ways for learners and mentors to network, create matches for themselves, and continue to assist with requests

# Design Decision 2: Schedule

Once you've determined the structure for your mentoring program, you will have to think about and create a program schedule. The type of schedule you choose will depend on your program's goals and structure. There are three main types of schedules: calendar-based, open, and programmatic.

- Calendar-based: As the name implies, these are programs that either run annually between set months or launch periodically and are set to run for a certain number of months.
- Open: This is an ongoing program. Once it is launched there is no expected end date for the program or the relationships formed within it.
- Programmatic: These programs are tied to other company initiatives or training events, and are not run on a set calendar timeframe.

## Calendar-Based

Calendar-based mentoring programs are either annual programs that last during a set timeframe (for example, February through October) or programs that last a certain amount of time (for example, a 14-month program).

Programs that are scheduled on an annual basis like this are the most common, because this reliable schedule is generally easiest for both learners and administrators. Learners and mentors will come to expect a certain rhythm from the year, and administrators can plan their workload in advance.

Calendar-based programs work well with all of the basic structures. It is a great option for hybrid structures, because keeping a straightforward schedule is a good idea if you're adding complexity to the structure. It will also be the best schedule for program goals related to annual company processes, such as performance reviews, high-potential or talent mapping, or individual development plans (IDP). The largest drawback to using a calendar-based program is the risk of leaving people out during any gaps between program cycles.

## Open

Open or ongoing programs are the all-night convenience store version of program schedules—anyone can join or leave the program at any time, which means that learners and mentors are able to "stop in" as time permits. This type of program schedule is less common than a calendar-based program because it requires a program administrator to be available year-round for onboarding participants into the program, assisting with matches, offboarding those leaving the program, supporting participants, and the many other tasks required to run a successful program. Without a program cycle, organizations with a large learner population may need to devote a full-time resource just to maintaining the program.

An open program schedule works best with mentor-led or peer-mentoring structures because it is sometimes easier to move individuals in and out of a group rather than facilitating new matches for traditional one-on-one relationships. However, the other structures can still work with an open schedule as long as you are confident that the program's administrative needs will be met.

## Programmatic

Programmatic schedules fit into the "other" category. Essentially, this schedule supports a mentoring program that is tied to some other organizational initiative (for example, launch of new core values), training class (for example, a new branch manager training class that occurs as needed), or strategy (for example, reorganizing departments).

Traditional or group-mentoring structures work much better with this kind of schedule because these initiatives tend to be about a group of expert leaders guiding those with less expertise. Mentoring programs that are tied to an event or program to reinforce something important to the organization also work well with the programmatic schedule.

The largest drawback to this type of schedule is that employees may see "flavor of the month" written all over it. In other words, a programmatic schedule is defined by being temporary, which may not always appeal to potential mentors and learners. To overcome this, make sure you have a plan for ongoing maintenance and support of the program.

## Design Decision 3: The Matching Process

Effective mentoring is based on credible and influential relationships, and playing matchmaker to create those relationships can be intimidating. There are many ways learners and mentors can find each other (Figure 3-11). This section covers the most common ones: self-selection, role and location, SME rotation, and skills match.

### Figure 3-11. Ways to Match Learners and Mentors

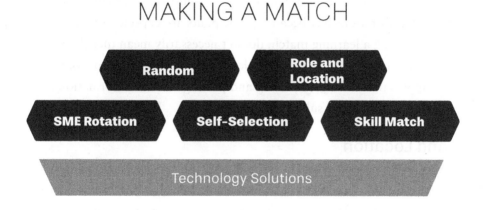

MAKING A MATCH

Random

Role and Location

SME Rotation

Self-Selection

Skill Match

Technology Solutions

### Self-Selection

What if learners and mentors can find each other? Given enough information, participants can seek each other out, which allows for more ownership in the process, and in some cases helps in overcoming the awkwardness that can occur when mentoring relationships are forced.

One way to facilitate self-selection is with a technology platform that automates the discovery and matching processes. Participants register in the system, which then matches them to potential mentors. Then participants can evaluate their matches using information mentors have uploaded into the system. This gives participants a feeling of ownership in the process, and also decreases the workload of program administrators, who might otherwise spend days or weeks in the matching process.

Aside from using a dedicated software program, you can also assist the self-selection process by posting relevant info about mentors on a protected intranet site. Or you could organize a mentoring program launch event with a speed-dating component so participants can find their best match—no technology needed.

Self-selection works well with all structures and schedules. For mentor-led and peer-mentoring programs, individuals usually don't need to know much information to sign up for a group. With traditional or reverse mentoring, learners and mentors will need more information about one another so they can make educated decisions about who they will be working with. However, that extra effort to gather and provide the relevant information can pay dividends, because self-selected relationships are often more organic than other types.

The two biggest factors in whether to choose this method of matching are:

- Culture: Is your organization's culture open, transparent, and egalitarian enough to promote individuals who want to find mentors across the entire business? In cultures that are heavily political or siloed, for example, a learner may feel pressure to choose a mentor for less-than-ideal reasons.
- Administration: Just because participants are expected to take ownership in finding a learning match, doesn't necessarily mean that there are fewer administrative needs. Unless you are using some sort of software application to help, gathering and posting relevant information for self-selection can be a substantial undertaking.

## Role and Location

One of the more common practices for matching learners and mentors is matching a learner with a mentor who is in a certain role, and (usually) geographically desirable. For example, a new salesperson will likely be mentored by an account executive (role) in the same office (location).

The benefit of this method is that program administrators have more control, and are able to make sure mentor resources are applied equally and effectively. However, the risks of putting the matching process entirely in the hands of administrators are:

- Artificial Relationships: Many participants express some concern about being matched with a total stranger, often complaining that the relationship feels forced.
- Effort: In very large programs, it takes a lot of time and effort to match everyone up effectively.

Although this method works well for all structures, it works especially well for traditional, reverse, and mentor-led groups. Because these relationships include experts as mentors, an administrator will want the most control over when those experts are leveraged in mentoring relationships.

Role and location is also a great matching method for open or ongoing programs. That way, when a new learner or mentor joins the program, the program administrator has a full view of potential matches for the individual. Overall, this method is most often chosen when the mentoring relationship is driven by specific content, such as a new hire onboarding program, sales preparatory program, or new manager leadership program.

## SME Rotation

One of the less common methods for matching learners and mentors is through a subject matter expert (SME) rotation. In this model, the learners are matched with a series of SMEs over a set period of time, so they can learn and practice specific skills.

This method can be very effective for programs in leadership development or for new supervisors. For example, a learner in a large company might be in a supervisory position that has six critical competencies she must work on during her first year on the job; however, the order does not matter. In a SME rotation, the learner would be assigned six different mentors who each excel in one of the competencies. She would participate in a two-month, one-on-one relationship with one SME mentor after the other, until she completed the program.

This method works best for the traditional structure. It would be challenging, but possible, to use a SME rotation for reverse or mentor-led groups. However, it doesn't work for a peer-led group because that method does not use an SME.

SME rotation is most easily leveraged for a calendar-based schedule, because all learners and mentors are open and available for matching. However, the other schedule styles also work well. This is a great matching method to use if your mentor pool is depleted and you need to stretch it out without asking too much of their time. SME rotation is also a great matching method if part of your program's goal is to increase the learner's network, because he will be exposed to a greater number of SMEs.

## Skills Match

While some programs are driven by specific content (new hire onboarding), other mentoring programs are established to help individuals develop their goals. In those programs, learners should be connected with mentors who are skilled in specific areas that will help them grow.

The skills match process is often done with a tool such as an individual development plan (IDP; see appendix F) to capture learner goals. This gives program administrators a snapshot of each learner's top areas to work on.

On the mentor side, administrators can use a variety of tools to find mentors that match the learner's IDP goals. For example, performance review or 9-box data show a mentor candidate's skills in key areas (appendix G). Surveys by mentors or supervisors, as well as 360-degree or multirater assessments, also provide valuable information about learner and mentor skills, how the learners view themselves, and how others perceive their behavior.

After program administrators have gathered the learner's IDP goals and performance data for mentors, they can begin matching learner needs to the available mentors who excel in those areas. Be aware that in large programs (for example, more than 100 learners), this is a very long and challenging process.

The skills matching process is involved and requires a lot of effort from program administrators, so it does not work well with open or ongoing schedules. It works best for peer-led groups because only learners with similar goals need to be matched, but it can also work with any other structure. Just remember, the more relationships (for example, a traditional structure), the more work takes to match everyone effectively.

One more warning: You will need a lot of mentors for this process, because you will want to find the best matches for each learner's needs.

## Random

Arbitrary assignment of learners to mentors is a viable option for programs with highly capable mentors. In general, if learners are seeking development in similar areas, and all mentors can effectively contribute to that development, this might be a reasonable choice. Another situation in which a random assignment occurs is in very small programs that do not have much choice.

But beware of mismatches! The risk in using a random assignment is that learners are not able to get what they need for growth because of a match with an unqualified mentor.

## Technology Solutions

There are a handful of applications on the market to help programs automate or streamline the matching process. Some stand-alone software platforms are databases that enable the online building of various mentor relationships. Additionally, some learning management systems include this functionality.

If you are trying to empower program participants to make their own matches, a technology solution can be an effective way to achieve that goal. However, software licenses are an added (and possibly unexpected) cost to your budget.

# Design Decision 4: Learner Participation

This is the point where you begin to dive into the real participant experience. Now that you have determined the shape of your program through structure, schedule, and matching process, it's time to get tactical with what you expect your learners to do.

Learner participation is designed using the three Es:

- Entry: How will learners get into the mentoring program?
- Exit: What are the different ways learners might leave the program?
- Expectations: What do you expect of your learners while they remain in the program?

## Learner Program Entry

Through your conversations with stakeholders during the alignment phase, you gathered information about how learners might participate in the program. Now you need to decide who will participate in the program. The important part of this step is ensuring that you have a clear understanding of the process, logistics, and administration required for program entry, based on the structure, schedule, and matching process. Here are some of the most common learner program entry methods:

- Target criteria: As part of the selected target group for the program (for example, new hire or high potential), the learner is invited to participate.
- Automatic entry: Any learner who wants to be a part of the program can participate. This method may include an application, which is used for matching purposes.
- Nomination: The learner must be chosen through a nomination process.
- Selection committee: When learners apply for the program their applications are reviewed by a committee. This is typically only used for high-potential or leadership programs.

## Learner Program Exit

One of the more overlooked aspects of designing a mentoring experience is thinking through how your learners might leave a program. This usually occurs due to reaching either the scheduled end of the program or the mentoring relationship duration. However, there are also many reasons someone might have to leave midprogram.

It is very important that you discuss the process for leaving before the program is launched, which will help avoid emergencies during the program itself. Once you identify a potential reason for someone exiting the program, make sure you determine how to handle it. The following are a few expected and unexpected ways in which a learner might exit the program:

- Expected exits:
  - scheduled program end
  - mentoring relationship planned end after a set time
  - graduation from program
  - self-elect out after accomplishing goals, making progress.
- Unexpected exits:
  - personal emergency or event
  - poor performance at work
  - failure to show progress or effort during mentoring relationship
  - failure to meet participation requirements.

## Learner Program Expectations

Once you know how learners will be entering and exiting your program, outline your expectations for their time in the program. Sometimes setting expectations can have a negative feel, so be careful to craft your language in a positive light. Figure 3-12 is an example set of expectations. Your program's structure, schedule, and goals will influence these expectations.

### Figure 3-12. Sample Learner Expectations Letter

This mentoring experience gives you access to expert guides from our organization to accelerate your development.

If issues arise that take your attention away from the mentoring relationship, or if you find you are no longer able to meet the expectations of this program, please contact the program administrator.

As part of this program, every participant must continue to demonstrate excellent performance on the job. If performance becomes an issue, you may be asked to step away from the program to concentrate on improving your job performance.

You will gain the most out of your time in this program by demonstrating a good faith effort toward achieving goals, being present and engaged for mentoring meetings, and taking ownership over your learning experience.

# Design Decision 5: Mentor Participation

Next, you have to take a long look at what you want your mentors to experience. Mentors are critical to the program's success. If you give mentors the best possible experience, they are more likely to continue supporting the program. As you did with learners, you should look at participation through the three Es:

- Entry: How will mentors get into the mentoring program?
- Exit: What are the different ways mentors might leave the program?
- Expectations: What do we expect of our mentors in the program?

## Mentor Program Entry

Once again, you will refer to your work in the alignment step of the model to review any notes from stakeholders about how mentors will be chosen for the program. In this step, you should strive for clarity about the process, logistics, and administration required for program entry. The most common program entry methods for mentors resemble those of the learner:

- Target criteria: Job role, skill, or performance expertise matching the goals of the program (for example, excellent employee development scores on reviews).
- Automatic entry: Any mentor who wants to be a part of the program can participate. This method may include an application, which will be used for matching purposes.
- Nomination: Mentors might be nominated by peers or supervisors who believe they are excellent mentors, guides, and coaches.
- Selection committee: Mentor applications to the program are reviewed by a selection committee. This method is used very rarely.

## Mentor Program Exit

Good mentors are almost always the busiest and most sought after individuals in the organization. While they may be excited to participate in a mentoring program, there are many reasons why they may have to unexpectedly leave. As with learners, you want to pay close attention to how and why this could happen, and how to handle it if it does. The goal is to minimize chaos caused by an unexpected exit, and to create the best experience possible for mentors. The following are a few examples of expected and unexpected exit options for mentors:

- Expected exits:
  - scheduled program end
  - mentoring relationship planned to end after a set time
  - self-elect out after helping a learner accomplish her goals or make progress.
- Unexpected exits:
  - personal emergency or event
  - poor performance at work
  - unreliable, late, or absent during mentoring meetings
  - failure to meet other participation requirements.

## Mentor Program Expectations

The final piece of the experience puzzle is setting expectations for a program's mentors. In most cases, the expectations you have for your mentors will not vary too much from those you've set for your learners, but it is important to be thorough and explicit. Figure 3-13 is a sample letter addressed to a mentor, which sets the expectations for the program.

### Figure 3-13. Sample Mentor Expectations Letter

Thank you for volunteering to be a mentor in this program. Your work will help the learner grow and develop, while giving you practice in key leadership skills.

If issues arise that take your attention away from the mentoring relationship, or if you find that you are no longer able to meet the expectations of this program, please contact the program administrator.

As a part of this program, every participant must continue to demonstrate excellent performance on the job. If performance becomes an issue, you may be asked to step away from the program to concentrate on improving your job performance.

You will gain the most from your time in this program by being present and engaged for all mentoring meetings, investing in the development of your learners, and proactively seeking self-development opportunities to hone your skills as a mentor.

## Pulling It All Together

After you've chosen a structure, made the schedule, selected the matching process, and determined the learner and mentor experiences, you have the initial design for a mentoring program that's unique to the needs and goals of your organization (Figure 3-14).

Let's continue looking at the sales team example from chapter 2, and review how the design decisions you made help shape your program. By using the purpose statement from the last chapter, along with your stakeholder feedback, you can begin making design decisions.

# Figure 3-14. Design Decisions Example

| | |
|---|---|
| Design Decision 1: **Structure** | **PRIMARY STRUCTURE = TRADITIONAL** Addresses the need for deep, trusting relationships that can propel an individual forward. ✚ **HYBRID = MENTOR-LED & PEER** To address common skills gaps as well as involve top leadership, frequent mentor-led groups will be used. To foster community and knowledge sharing, peer group will be used. |
| Design Decision 2: **Schedule** | **CALENDAR-BASED** The entire program will kick off in March and continue for six months. One-on-one relationships are matched from the start. A mentor-led group will meet once per month; the first three months they will be led by a mentor with a specific skill set, and then will transition to a second mentor for the back half of the program. The peer group will determine when and how often they want to meet. |
| Design Decision 3: **Matching** | **SELF-SELECT, NOMINATION** Learners in the program will complete IDPs and will be provided with a list of mentors with relevant info, such as resumes and bios. Learners will select their own one-on-one mentor. Senior leadership will choose individual mentors for the mentor-led group. Mentors for one-on-one relationships may volunteer or be nominated and vetted by committee. |
| Design Decision 4: **Learner Participation** | **ENTRY**: All members of the sales team will participate in the program. **EXIT**: Program end scheduled for August. Also, individuals may self-select out for any reason with approval from supervisor. (Process defined further as needed.) **EXPECTATIONS**: Continue to meet performance goals, progress toward developmental goals, be present and respectful during mentoring meetings. |
| Design Decision 5: **Mentor Participation** | **ENTRY**: Nominated mentors will be vetted by a chosen committee; some mentors will be invited by committee to address specific skill needs. **EXIT**: Program end scheduled for August. Also, individuals may self-select out for any reason. (Process defined further as needed.) **EXPECTATIONS**: Be present and respectful during mentoring meetings, invest in the developmental growth of those assigned, share expertise and encourage individual problem solving. |

# How to Match the Experience to the Organization

Elaine Biech, President, ebb associates inc

Could a traditional 60-year-old organization that had never had a formal employee develop-ment program create a successful mentoring program? The talent manager believed it could. She had been on the job no more than two months when she presented the idea to the CEO, who had placed her in the position. The CEO was also relatively new, but he was aware that the culture had a limited development mindset. He encouraged the talent manager to move forward and do all she could to better align the departments in the organization.

## Key to Success: Buy-In

Although the talent manager did not need anyone's approval to initiate the effort, she knew that without the support of the organization's senior leaders, the program would not succeed. One of her first tasks was to create a talent management board (TMB) of key leaders repre-senting the organization's major departments.

When she first presented the idea for a mentoring program to the board, their initial response was to scoff at the idea. After all, nearly half of the organization's employees had PhDs, including new hires; why would they need a mentor? Still, the talent manager pressed her point with several finely tuned and pointed questions:

- What causes the greatest problems for new hires?
- What concerns do you have about promotions?
- If we were to implement a mentoring program, what guidance would you offer?

The talent manager knew that she needed buy-in from the TMB for the program to be a success. So at the next meeting, she presented a report summarizing the previous discussion to demonstrate that she recognized their needs and concerns. She also included input from the HR department. The highlights of this report are listed in the sidebar on the next page.

One of the lingering issues the talent manager noticed was that the organization's senior managers believed that smart people could find their own mentors informally. However, while interviews with 50 of the organization's best and brightest revealed that 91 percent agreed or agreed strongly that they needed a mentor, 86 percent had done nothing about it. Why? Some of the reasons given included:

- not enough time
- don't know how to start
- too shy or proud
- can't figure out who could help me
- afraid to make a mistake and not know how to end it if necessary
- need help being objective in my selection; it can't be my friend
- supervisor might see having a mentor as a negative, which would affect my performance appraisal.

## Purpose and Considerations to Initiate a Formal Mentoring Program

TMB Concerns

- New employees don't understand organizational politics
- We employ bright people, but they aren't familiar with other parts of the organization
- Leaders are busy and shouldn't be responsible for another task: mentoring
- Managers, scientists, and engineers would need to learn how to mentor
- There is often no place for new hires to move up, and when they do receive a promotion, they're often not prepared

TMB Desires and Expectations

- There should be enough mentors: we have many smart people
- Branch offices need to be involved
- Need to maintain a personal touch throughout the program

HR Comments

- A mentoring program will help attract and retain good employees
- It could be a way to reward or retain high-potential candidates
- Thus far, supervisor development has been lacking
- An aging workforce is creating a sense of urgency to transfer their knowledge to the younger generation
- Leaders do not know people in other departments or throughout the organization
- There are not enough rotational opportunities

Sharing the data and comments with the TMB (as well as allowing time for them to get used to the idea), led to emphatic approval for the program and an admonishment of, "What's taking so long!"

As the talent manager started to move forward she had to combat a consultant she'd hired to help design the program. The consultant's model was one in which employees were required to interview at least three senior leaders and then choose a mentor from there. The talent manager and her program coordinator did not believe this was feasible for the organization—they believed that mentors and learners should complete a short application, which the talent coordinator would use to match individuals in a partnership based on the knowledge, skills, and attitude required by the learner.

## The Plan

Although the program did not have a formal charter, the talent manager used guidance from the TMB minutes to define how the program would operate and what it hoped to accomplish.

The organization supported a traditional approach to mentoring in which a single learner was matched with a single mentor, based on criteria of what the learner needed most. The goal was to ensure that more internal candidates were ready for promotions when positions became available. The mentor served many roles, including consultant, adviser, challenger, orchestrator, and coach. One of the TMB members wanted to use a matching platform that his daughter's company used to match pairs, but this was voted down by the group. The final TMB guidance included:

- Operating Direction
    - The talent manager is responsible for the overall operations and budget.
    - The program coordinator, who reports to the talent manager, is responsible for the day-to-day operations and matching mentors and learners.
    - Develop a mentoring guide, which explains the mentor's job and the learner's responsibilities. It should also include characteristics of successful mentors and learners, suggestions for developmental activities, an example of a partnership agreement, communication guidelines, and tips to make the relationship work.
    - Mentors and learners will complete a simple application form.
    - The program coordinator will match mentors and learners.
- Guidelines for Mentors and Learners
    - Mentors shall not be in the direct line of supervision (he can't be your boss's boss).
    - Mentors shall not be more than two steps up the chain.
    - Matched pairs (partnerships) must maintain the relationship for a full year.
    - All mentor partners will meet at least once a month.
    - Learners must have a signature approval from their supervisors to participate.
    - Learners must accept responsibility in taking the lead to schedule meetings, identify discussion topics, ask for support, and any other actions that make the relationship successful.
    - The partners should use the learner's IDP as a discussion starter.
    - Mentors and learners will receive training prior to starting the program.
    - Mentors and learners should complete a partnership agreement that defines their objectives, responsibilities, and expectations.
    - Every high-potential employee is required to have a mentor.
    - Any employee can request a mentor (with supervisor approval).
    - Anyone leaving the program must schedule an exit interview with the talent manager to explain the circumstances.
    - Employees working in the six field offices must be able to participate.

After the first year of the program, changes were made to accommodate the organization's needs. The original plan scheduled an annual matchup event that brought mentors and learners together for the first time and included a training component. However, after the program began seeing positive results, employees who had initially been reluctant to participate clamored to get involved and to find a mentor. To accommodate the requests, the program coordinator decided to instead make matches throughout the year. Rather than have a single event each year, the program coordinator matched learners and mentors as they applied and then gave them a training overview in the selected mentor's office, leaving the newly formed partners to begin to develop their partnership agreement.

The training manager and program coordinator also began scheduling quarterly special events for the mentors and learners, which included guest speakers, panel discussions, unique training, field trips, and meetings with senior management called "Whine and Cheese." The most popular presentation was The Baby Boomer Meets the Millennial.

## Was the Program Successful?

The mentoring program was considered a success and is still in existence today. Success was measured in several ways, including measurements at Levels 1 and 3, and an informal Level 4 measurement. Here are the highlights of each:

- Level 1 included a semiannual and annual survey of mentors and learners. The goal was to see a satisfaction rating better than 93 percent. Suggestions for improvement were incorporated into the program whenever possible. Goals were met every year.
- Level 3 involved interviews with the learners' supervisors to determine if the learner was transferring any of the skills, knowledge, and, in some cases, changed attitudes to the job. The goal of 90 percent success was met every year except the first one.
- Level 4 examined the retention rate of high potentials, as well as the promotion rate of all learners. The talent manager used data from the previous five years as a baseline, and the results showed that the increase for each was close to 25 percent per year. While no numeric goals were established initially, in the program's third year a 50 percent goal was set for both measures. Even though the 50 percent goal was never achieved, it encouraged the talent team to stretch expectations, and by the fifth year, the program was able to achieve a 49 percent increase.
- Operational and TMB expectations were all met, including:
  - Ensure there are enough mentors.
  - Provide training for mentors and learners.
  - Maintain enthusiasm in the program.

## Brilliant Accidents

The TMB could not have predicted the importance and value of each program element. The following brilliant accidents were decisions that led to results that were more positive than expected:

- Mentoring guide. Mentors and learners alike used the mentoring guide to get started. But the real value occurred when employees asked to join the program midway through the year. The guide provided all the necessary resources, allowing mentor and learner partnerships to be formed year-round, with just-in-time training. Luckily the TMB had insisted that the talent manager and her team create a mentoring guide right from the start.

- Celebrate mentors. At the end of the first year, the program coordinator asked the CEO to sign thank-you notes she had written to the mentors. The CEO not only signed the notes, but added his own personal message to each. The notes are valued by everyone who receives them.

- Use the IDP. Using the IDP as the foundation of the mentoring program spilled over into developmental discussions between supervisors and their employees. Once both mentors and employees saw the value in the IDP document, it came to be viewed as a worthwhile tool, not just something to do.

- Never say never. The TMB made it clear that they only wanted to have a traditional-type mentoring program. However, following one of the special events, The Baby Boomer Meets the Millennial, one of the TMB members wanted a Millennial to mentor him about a variety of items. This was the start of the reverse–traditional mentoring hybrid model.

- Don't underestimate your success. Between the initial matchup and the additional participants who wanted to get involved midyear, the program almost doubled its original involvement objectives. Thanks to the mentoring program's excellent reputation, whenever the program coordinator asked someone to consider being a mentor, she received an affirmative response.

- Program coordinators will be busy. Assigning one person as the program coordinator was one of the best ideas. She knew at least half of the employees in the organization. And if she didn't know someone with specific skills and personal traits, she knew someone whom she could ask for a recommendation. This was critical, given that the anticipated number of people in the program was almost twice what the organization expected.

- Make success the learners' responsibility. This guideline originated with the TMB's belief that the mentors would be too busy for added responsibility. It turned out to be the biggest gift to the program, resulting in two valuable outcomes: First, it was easy to get mentors to volunteer because the task seemed less formidable. Second, it forced the learners to take a leadership role, overcome their shyness, and accept responsibility for their own success.

The successes of the mentoring program in this traditional organization demonstrate that it can be done anywhere. You need to plan for a structure that aligns with the culture, clearly define roles and responsibilities for the mentors and learners, and select an operating process that will be accepted and supported by the organization. Putting these fundamental elements in place before you launch is your key to success.

# Conclusion

After the sometimes challenging work of the alignment phase, the designing the experience phase provides tangible progress in building an effective mentoring program. This is when your program begins to take shape through your design decisions about the structure, schedule, and matching process.

After the design foundation is in place, use learner and mentor participation to add texture to the experience. This allows you to dive deep into your plan for how program participants can enter and exit the program, and the expectations they must meet while participating.

But the design stage is just the beginning. The next step is to determine how you will launch the program.

### Key Insights: Design the Experience

1. Starting with design (instead of alignment) is likely to result in a program that fails.
2. Consider how your organization's culture might influence design decisions. What preconceived notions might already exist?
3. The first design decision is program structure. Will you use a traditional, reverse, mentor-led, or peer group approach? Or will you use a hybrid approach?
4. Informal mentoring, or social learning, has tremendous potential for talent development, but may require some purposeful design work to take hold in your organization.
5. The second design decision is how to schedule the program. Will it be on a calendar-based, always open, or programmatic schedule?
6. The third design decision involves choosing a matching process for the mentoring relationships. Remember that some options work better with some structures than others.
7. Once the program is well defined, the fourth design decision is determining the learner experience with entry, exit, and expectations during the program.
8. The fifth and final design decision is to choose the mentor experience in program entry, exit, and expectations.
9. Incorporating feedback from across the organization will not only create buy-in for the program, but also ensure cultural alignment in the participant experience.
10. When designing the experience, you need to consider every aspect of the learner and mentor experience. This will lead to greater satisfaction with the program.

# Chapter Exercises

## Program Charter

Use the program charter template in appendix B to draft a design (or redesign) of your mentoring program. Begin with the alignment work from chapter 2 (purpose statement). You'll add in the additional elements—such as program launch, success measures, and support plans—in the coming chapters. Once you have a draft completed (either individually or with your working team), meet with at least two stakeholders to get feedback.

# 4

# Launch the Program

If you could get up the courage to begin,
you have the courage to succeed.
—David Viscott

## Launch and Relaunch

Ready, set, go! In most talent development solution projects, such as workshops and training sessions, all of the work leads up to a pilot or launch for that solution. This is another way in which formal mentoring programs are quite different from other talent development options. For mentoring programs, launch events are not the goal of the project; they are simply the gateway to success.

Even though a lot of effort has been invested before participants are even aware of the program, the program launch is the point at which learners and mentors first experience the program. It is when they register, access resources, and gain key information and skills that will help shape a positive and successful experience during the rest of the mentoring program.

A mentoring program launch or kickoff can take many forms, depending on your specific situation. For programs that are calendar-based and just getting started, plan a launch event that can be replicated each program cycle. For new, open-ended programs, you will need to either hold regular launch events or create an asynchronous onboarding experience. In other situations, the best approach might be a soft launch, where only the minimum viable product is piloted, with a plan to iteratively improve the result.

Many programs that were not initially successful are relaunched after the design is improved. For these programs, the launch may focus more on repairing a broken reputation by serving as a marketing medium where program leaders can explain important improvements to the program.

The launch event for your mentoring program needs to be as carefully thought out as each of the other design aspects in the AXLES model. You will want to approach the launch of the mentoring program with certain considerations in mind, such as participant needs, scalability, and design decisions.

# Considerations

In some ways, designing a mentoring program launch is like designing an entire talent development project within another project. You should think carefully about what your audience needs, and the outcomes you want from the experience. It's also important to consider the same design elements as you would in a more traditional training program or workshop.

## What Do Participants Need at the Beginning of This Program Cycle?

Fortunately, you have already spent a considerable amount of time thinking about participant needs throughout the AXLES model. By now, you should have an idea to start with regarding what learners and mentors need during the program launch. Here are some factors to consider:

- mentor skills development
- learner skills development
- program purpose and outcomes
- encouragement from past mentors
- experiences of past learners
- clarification of processes and procedures
- mentor expectations
- learner expectations
- available resources
- relationships matching
- expectations for feedback, review, and assessment
- creation of a community of practice.

The needs you discover will guide your decisions about which launch components should be included, and how those components can be best developed to reach needed outcomes.

## What Is the Impact of Future Scalability and Schedules on the Program Launch?

This consideration goes back to the decisions about structure and schedule you made during the Design the Experience step of the AXLES model. Certain program structures and schedules will have a considerable impact on the design of the program launch; Table 4-1 provides a few examples.

## Table 4-1. Structure and Schedule Factors on Program Launch

| Structure | |
|---|---|
| One-on-One | First opportunity for relationship matches, schedule first meetings, set expectations for the learner and mentor roles, establish relationship goals |
| Reverse | Share program purpose, explain the match process, clarify roles, set relationship goals |
| Mentor-Led Groups | Hold first group meeting, share background and establish relationships, discuss group learning and performance goals |
| Peer Mentoring | Set communication guidelines, establish relationships, discuss learning and performance goals |
| Schedule | |
| Open | Recurring launches throughout program cycle to include new participants |
| Calendar-Based | Recurring launches for each program cycle, with launch events required or optional for former participants |
| Programmatic | Launches based on the needs of the associated initiative or program; all attendees have equal access to launch events and resources |

Additionally, your mentoring program may be targeting a subset of the talent in your organization, with the intent to eventually scale up and include more people. In that case, any mentoring program launch event should be developed with a mind toward how reproducible it is.

You should also consider whether the design can accommodate larger populations. For example, a face-to-face, all-day program launch may be ideal for a group of 30 employees who all work out of a single location; but, if next year that program includes 200 additional employees who are geographically dispersed, that launch design will cost significantly more.

Of course, it can be appropriate to go all out with the first program launch (or relaunch) and celebrate with an event that purposefully takes more resources or will be difficult to reproduce in the future. If you want the first launch to have a large impact, make sure you plan for future launches to cost less or require fewer resources. What's important is that you discuss this with your project sponsor and together make an intentional design decision.

## How Should You Deliver the Event?

How can you best reach your mentors and learners? You will want to tailor the launch event to your participants' preferences and where they're located. The following are some basic considerations for delivery methods. Your program and organization will likely have a few other factors that also influence the design of your program launch.

## Geographic Location

Are the participants in your mentoring program all in the same location, or are they spread out around the country? If they're all in the same location, a face-to-face event works well. Unless a budget has been allocated for travel, dispersed participants generally make a virtual event necessary.

## Bandwidth and Availability

We've all heard that all-too-common constraint of, "They're too busy to come to a meeting." If the participants do not have enough bandwidth to dedicate to a longer live event, consider making it asynchronous (self-paced) or break it up into small pieces and roll it out over time. This also works for participants who are traveling a lot for their jobs or don't have much control over their availability, such as salespeople.

## Learning Experience Preference

The audiences in your organization will generally have preferences regarding professional development. Some prefer live face-to-face events, while others would rather have videos, resources, and documents that they can access any time. It's up to you to figure out which methods your participants prefer and then tailor the event to them.

## Senior Leadership Availability

Ask a senior leader to speak to a live group of virtual or face-to-face mentor participants. The senior leader's credibility and sponsorship will go a long way to inspire and motivate participants. If you have a willing and available leader, find a way to incorporate her into a live event. Or, see if she will record a video that you can use for future program launches.

## Program Schedule

Is your mentoring program following a traditional schedule, or is it more open? If the program has an open schedule in which participants join and leave the program on an ongoing basis, you'll need to schedule program launches either regularly as live events or as an asynchronous solution.

## Administrative Resources

The amount of administrative effort that is available has a large influence on how complex the program launch can be. For example, do administrators have the skills and time to create online communities, set up panels for a live program launch, run a series of virtual web conferencing meetings, or any of the other many possibilities of a mentoring program launch? The less bandwidth administrators have, the more streamlined the launch will have to be, and the more value participants will need to get from the slimmed-down experience.

# Communicate, Communicate, Communicate

The one non-negotiable aspect of a program launch is clear and thorough communication before, during, and after the event. No matter the shape your program launch event takes, participants should always feel informed.

## Prelaunch Communication

It is usually a good idea to get the word out about the program to your target learners and mentors well before it begins. You can use existing resources, such as newsletters, intranet sites, online communities, or internal social media, to get people excited about the upcoming program.

Prelaunch communications should include the program purpose statement so potential learners and mentors understand what the program intends to achieve. They can also include anecdotes or encouragement—in the form of a short video, audio or podcast message, or letter—from senior leaders who are championing the program. Additionally, depending on the design and timeline of the program, prelaunch communications may provide registration instructions for interested learners and mentors.

## Launch Communication

Right before the mentor program launches, or during the launch event, you will want to give everyone a welcome guide (see page 131), as well as instructions to complete any assessments or matching documents necessary to begin the program.

## Post-Launch Communication

No matter how well you discussed the next steps and what to expect from the program during the launch event, it is still important to reinforce that information with follow-up communications. You may want to send a reminder email with specific steps and upcoming due dates. Another option (usually for small groups) is send email calendar appointments to learners and mentors for milestone dates.

Finally, be sure to include the program administrator's contact information and any available resources on every communication that goes out about your mentoring program. Remember, mentoring relationships are occurring outside a classroom, not under the watchful eye of the talent development function. You want to constantly remind participants where they can find help and resources.

# Choosing Your Launch Design

Once you have determined which factors influence the design decisions of the mentoring program launch, it's time to begin designing the event itself. In this section, you will find many ideas that can be combined for the best possible launch experience for your mentors and learners. Each design idea includes a description and a note about when it is best applied or avoided.

Most of these ideas can be used effectively in either face-to-face or virtual launch environments, although not always equally well. In addition, each idea is a starting point. With some thought and creativity, you can use these concepts as a starting place for a cohesive and innovative program launch. However, keep in mind that any decision to include a launch component should be driven by how well it helps prepare participants to meet expectations and see success throughout the program.

## Informational Session

A good program launch delivers critical information—such as the program's purpose, how success is measured, relationship structures, and program expectations—to both learners and mentors. You should devote at least a short time in any launch session to explaining these concepts and allowing for participant questions and clarification.

However, just because you're sharing basic information, there's still room for you to get creative. For example, during a face-to-face session, set up a program information scavenger hunt and have pairs of participants look through their program materials to find answers to key questions. Have a prize ready for the winners. Another alternative to a boring talking head approach is to have participants interview senior leaders during the program launch, and then answer questions on a program information worksheet.

## Registration

Some programs allow interested participants to register at the launch event. This works well for open programs with a totally voluntary (everyone accepted) program entrance policy. In these cases, you will want to get potential participants excited about the program using communications leading up to the event. Your goal is for a large number of learners and mentors attend the launch event and register, because on-site registration is only a success if enough people show up and sign up. This idea also works well for programs with an open schedule, because they are designed to accommodate all talent in the organization.

However, on-site registration is not a good choice when the mentoring program has been designed with a specific focus, such as leadership development, that targets certain learner and mentor groups as candidates.

Program registration can also happen digitally, so with enough planning it can be included as part of a virtual launch process. This is especially true of virtual launches that are sequenced over time, instead of one longer session.

## Mentorship Matching

Depending on program structure, the matches between learners and mentors can be arranged during the launch event. This process works if the launch event is either a live event of significant length (at least several hours) or a series of events during which learners and mentors have time to find a good match.

In general, a face-to-face program launch is a great place for learners to self-select mentors in a one-to-one or group structure. With some planning, this approach can also work with other types of programs, such as peer groups. If matching is done in any way other than self-selection, you will find it challenging to conduct matching on-site, given the risk of participants not attending.

However, there are many obstacles that prevent on-site matching from working well. For example, what if you don't have a good mentor to learner ratio? What if there aren't enough mentors with the right skill sets? What if learners aren't happy with their on-site choices? Instead, the matching process is better before the launch event for all types of programs except self-selection.

## Assessment Debriefs

Many formal mentoring programs use assessments to help the matching process or prepare participants to make the most of their mentoring relationships. Using time during the mentoring program launch to give a group debrief of assessments is a great way to prepare participants for the experience they are about to have.

Typically, these assessments—multiraters, communication-style indicators, and leadership-style indicators—help create awareness about key areas of strength and development for learners and mentors. Each specific assessment tool is a window into a specific group of behaviors. A multirater tool provides information about a learner's self-perception and the perceptions of his team and supervisor. Communication- and leadership-style assessment tools provide insights into the learner's and mentor's natural behavioral tendencies and areas for improvement. These assessments are a powerful resource for both learners and mentors, and add a lot of value to the launch experience.

It's best to use the same assessments the organization is already using; for example, if the organization uses a multirater assessment tool through its learning management system, use that assessment method because participants are likely already be familiar with it. Provide links to the assessments before the launch event so that the assessment results can be debriefed as a group.

Group debriefs, which usually show you how to read the results of the assessment and what to do with them, work equally well either face-to-face or virtually. Another way to increase the value of the assessment debrief is to have pairs of participants (either matched learners and mentors or randomly assigned partners) identify action items from the assessment report.

## Development Plans and Goal Setting

One of the most challenging aspects of a mentoring relationship is setting realistic and actionable development and performance goals. In most effective programs, these goals serve as the baseline for measuring growth (chapter 5). You can devote a small portion of your launch event to giving participants—both mentors and learners—tips for how to set appropriate goals, as well as demonstrating how mentoring conversations can address those goals.

This works very well in all launch event formats, even asynchronous onboarding. For programs that are open and inclusive, it is important to demonstrate a diverse range of goal examples that cater to your wide spectrum of learners. For programs with more specific and targeted content, you may even provide a list of goals that learners can choose from and adapt to their needs. For example, in a leadership development program, you may suggest, "Increase my knowledge of the business by seeking opportunities to interact with other departments."

To get the most out of this work, you should provide time for participants to put what they learned into action and get feedback on their goals.

## Participant Panel

An exciting experience for learners and mentors who are new to the mentoring program is to watch a panel discussion by former mentors and learners. Delivered either face-to-face or virtually, the panel discussion could feature four to six individuals answering questions about their experience in the program. You will want to select panelists carefully and prepare some questions in advance, in case the audience is slow to warm up. To learn more about panels, see this chapter's case study.

## Mentor Skills Workshop

Many people have the desire, but not necessarily the skills, to be an effective mentor. Fortunately, mentors typically request help growing their mentoring skill sets. The program launch is a great place to do that, if enough time is allotted. If your launch event is live, you can start working on mentor skills development on-site, and then continue your work throughout the program cycle. Focus on key roles mentors should play, as well as effective versus ineffective behaviors mentors can use to help learners with their development. (We'll discuss this in more depth in chapter 6.)

## Learner Skills Workshop

Learners also need advice on being coachable and open to mentor guidance. Use the program launch to begin a discussion about the best way learners can approach their roles and get the most out of their mentoring relationships. Just like the mentor skills workshop, developing learner skills is something that is best started at the launch event and continued throughout the mentoring program. Learners also need to understand their responsibilities within the program, as well as the skills and behaviors they should use to get the most out of their mentoring relationship.

## Other Resources

The possibilities are endless when it comes to potential components for the mentoring program launch, including video clips of senior leaders acting as promoters and champions of the program, readings that examine key skills or are motivational, icebreaker activities, and team trust exercises. Overall, the most important point is that you choose methods that best address your participants' needs and prepare them for their mentoring experiences.

# Launch Sequence

The goal of a mentoring program launch is to align your participants' needs with the program experience design. It is important to think of the program launch as part of the program experience, and not an isolated event. Figures 4-1 to 4-3 present three different program launch designs, demonstrating a wide spectrum of possibilities.

## Figure 4-1. Leadership Development Mentoring Program

| Launch Item | Details |
| --- | --- |
| Considerations | **Participant Needs:** Mentors and learners will want detailed information about participating in the program, the required level of effort, the schedule, and how much time is required. Mentors have the necessary industry expertise, but little experience with effective mentoring.<br><br>**Structure and Schedule Needs:** One-on-one program for about 60 learners and mentors, which will run annually from February to October.<br><br>**Delivery Factors:** Participants are geographically dispersed, but prefer face-to-face events. A budget is set aside for travel when needed. |

## Figure 4-1. Leadership Development Mentoring Program (cont.)

| Launch Item | Details |
|---|---|
| Prelaunch Communication | Communication-style assessments were sent to all participants, and individual development plans were sent to learners one month prior to the program launch. These are due back to program administrators a week prior to launch.<br><br>Prelaunch communications have outlined program details, participation expectations, and the program's purpose. A virtual informational webinar with Q&A is scheduled a week prior to launch. |
| Matching | Program administrators conducted a matching process using the completed assessments prior to launch event. |
| Program Launch Design | A full-day, face-to-face launch workshop was held at corporate headquarters.<br><br>8–8:45 a.m. — Welcome, Icebreaker Activity<br>8:45–9:30 a.m. — Goal-Setting Practice<br>9:30–10 a.m. — Matches Unveiled<br>**BREAK**<br>10:15–11:30 a.m. — Guided First Meetings<br>11:30 a.m.–12:30 p.m. — Social Networking Lunch<br>12:30–1:30 p.m. — Participant Panel<br>1:30–2 p.m. — Q&A With Program Administrators<br>**BREAK**<br>2:15–4:15 p.m. — Mentor and Learner Skills Workshops<br>**BREAK**<br>4:30–5 p.m. — Next Steps and Conclusion |

## Figure 4-2. Sales Onboarding Mentoring Program

| Launch Item | Details |
|---|---|
| Considerations | **Participant Needs:** Learners are new salespeople, so they will be concerned about how to be successful. They will be excited for the program, and most concerned about how to get what they need quickly to improve in their job.<br><br>**Structure and Schedule Needs:** One-on-one program that runs twice annually to onboard on average 15 new salespeople, mentored by senior salespeople in their office.<br><br>**Delivery Factors:** Even though mentor matches are in the same location, the program launch event must be virtual so that it is available to salespeople across offices. Because the learners are also new salespeople, they are typically filling their calendars with client meetings, and may not be able to set aside a predetermined time for a launch webinar. |
| Prelaunch Communication | Prelaunch communication outlined program details, participation expectations, the program's purpose, and sales performance milestones. Additional suggested resources were also sent, such as templates for territory review and other performance-related information. |
| Program Launch Design | The program launched with a live, half-hour virtual event, which was mostly informational. Following the live event, mentors and learners met in their own locations to establish the goals for their mentoring relationship. For three weeks following the program launch, both learners and mentors received email communications with additional helpful resources, suggestions on structuring mentoring conversations, and sales-specific readings and videos. |

## Figure 4-3. Employee Engagement Mentoring Program

| Launch Item | Details |
| --- | --- |
| Considerations | **Participant Needs:** Participants will need information about the program schedule, structure, and requirements. They will want to get the most out of their experience and need help setting goals.<br><br>**Structure and Schedule Needs:** Peer-mentoring structure with an open schedule. Expected participation is an average of 200 people.<br><br>**Delivery Factors:** Participants are geographically dispersed, with varying degrees of availability, titles, and backgrounds. The overall mentoring program does not have a large budget, so very little money has been allocated to the launch event. Most participants are comfortable with online conference software and other applications that might be used. |
| Prelaunch Communication | Prelaunch communications outlined program details, participation expectations, and the program's purpose. Additional suggested resources were also sent out, including the link to a multirater assessment. |
| Program Launch Design | A series of virtual webinars with predetermined agendas. Each was recorded and made available to accommodate busy schedules.<br><br>**Week 1:** Informational webinar and Q&A with former participants. (The first year has a panel with senior leaders and strong mentors.) Week 1 also included the link to an intranet portal where participants could register for their peer groups.<br><br>**Week 2:** Setting individual goals, which included examples, partner activities, and participant shares to the large group.<br><br>**Week 3:** Introducing group dynamics and managing peer groups. This content helped peer groups determine how to best structure themselves, the roles that were needed, and expectations for operating in a group.<br><br>**Week 4:** The final week of launch looked at developing yourself and others. This week's topic focused on how individuals can get the most impact from their experience in the group, and how they can best serve their peers in their development. |

# The After-Party

The biggest take away from this chapter is to think of your mentoring program launch not as an end to your development work, but as the first in a series of mentoring experiences for your participants. Give considerable thought to any follow-up communications and resources you send after the official launch of your mentoring program. Providing skill-specific tools, online videos, or a series of webinars will help renew participant motivation and keep program engagement high.

The launch event is also the first opportunity for learners and mentors to feel as though they are participating in a mentoring community. The more support they believe they have—from program administrators, senior leaders, and other participants—the more likely they are to have a positive experience.

# Launch to Create Momentum:
# Mentoring Panel Best Practices

Jeanne Masseth, CEO, Legacy Talent Development

A successful launch event can spark and inspire a rich mentoring relationship. It's often the first training experience mentors and learners will have on how to be successful in their roles, so it's critical that their experience is relevant and practical. A robust panel discussion with past mentoring experts is often very well received in launch events. Oftentimes the panelists' stories reinforce key mentoring concepts the facilitator has already made. They bring real-life, practical tips for participants, while answering questions about the mentoring process.

Mentoring panelists should be former successful mentors and learners (internal or external) who have been where your participants are: at the beginning of a great partnership. Invite approximately four to six individuals who have experienced formal mentoring and can share positive comments about the process. Be selective—a mix of former learners and mentors, male and female panelists, and multiple generations is optimal. Call each potential panelist to extend the invite, explain details, and cover logistics—they'll be speaking for five to 10 minutes about their mentoring experience, including building a solid relationship, overcoming challenges, and developing best practices. Then confirm all the logistics in an email, and request a short bio that you can use for their introduction.

During the launch event, set up the panelists at a table in the front of the room. Make sure you bring preprinted table tents with panelist names and a glass or bottle of water for each panelist. During the presentation, keep notes on key information the panelists share, which you may be able to integrate into your next launch event. In addition, take note of how the panelists relate to the audience to help you determine whom to invite to future discussions. At the conclusion of the discussion, you can present each panelist with a small gift or token of appreciation, and then follow that up with a handwritten thank-you note.

The panel flows nicely in the launch agenda right after lunch. It re-energizes the group with fresh faces and perspectives. Begin with panelist introductions using the bios they provide, and then ask them to present their mentoring stories, tips, and words of inspiration. Encourage participants to ask questions of any or all of the panelists. Allow approximately 30 minutes for the panelists' presentations, followed by 20 minutes of Q&A. The entire panel discussion can be facilitated in less than an hour.

Generating solid questions immediately following the presentation is vital, because one question is often a catalyst for the next. To ensure participants are ready with questions, ask them to prepare at least one question prior to the panel discussion. Here's one way you can do this: During the first morning break of launch training, place notecards or sticky notes at each table. When mentors and learners return from break, say that they probably have a lot of questions about the year ahead, and ask them to jot down at least one (or more) burning question they would like to ask someone who has been in their shoes as a new mentor or learner. Encourage them to continue jotting down questions as you cover more content.

Key questions mentors and learners may have include:

- What did you gain from the experience?
- How did you approach challenges or setbacks throughout the year?
- What were key moments or turning points in the mentoring relationship?
- How did you go about setting development goals and objectives?
- How do pairs on different schedules or in different locations connect?
- Did your relationship change over time?
- What is the most important piece of advice you have for a new mentor or learner?
- What do you wish you would've known at the outset of your relationship?

# Conclusion

When you launch the program for the first time, or relaunch it after revisions, you have an opportunity to set the stage for a positive and impactful mentoring experience for your learners and mentors. The communications that participants receive leading up to the program launch, and the experience they have during the launch event, is their introduction to how their mentoring experience should go.

Through careful planning, using specific considerations of the participant needs, you can design a launch event, or series of events, that provides critical information, supports community, and motivates participants to engage with their mentoring relationships at a high level. The most important idea of the mentoring program launch is to be mindful of the extended mentoring experience—use the launch as a gateway to the development that is possible within the mentoring program.

# Chapter Exercises

## Designing the Program Launch

Together with your project sponsor and project team, review the three considerations outlined in this chapter to determine the best method for launching your mentoring program:

- What do participants need at the beginning of this program cycle?
- What is the impact of future scalability and schedules on the program launch?
- How should you deliver the event?

## Program Launch Agenda

Using the responses to the questions above, and the template provided in appendix C, design your program launch. Remember, your design should meet the needs of your participants and focus on providing a positive experience.

### Key Insights: Program Launch

1.  The launch (or relaunch) of a formal mentoring program is not the end result of design work, but the beginning of the mentor and learner experience in your program.
2.  The program launch agenda is first determined by the needs of your participants.
3.  The mentoring program's structure and schedule, which you determined in the designing the experience step, influences the format of the program launch. Choose the format that will be most effective for the participants.
4.  Your organization's cultural preferences and constraints also affect design choices for the program launch.
5.  Spend some time planning what communications will go out to program participants before the program launches, during the launch event, and afterward to reinforce important information.
6.  Choose program components that add to your participants' experience while achieving necessary outcomes, such as skills training or informational sessions.
7.  Depending on your program's purpose and design, participants may be registered before or during the launch event.
8.  Self-selected mentor matching can happen during the launch event if it aligns to your program's purpose and intended outcomes.
9.  Use the sample launch event agendas included in this chapter to plan your mentoring program launch.
10. Consider including a robust panel discussion with mentoring experts or former mentoring program participants to help create a community experience for your program.

# Evaluate Effectiveness

However beautiful the strategy, you should occasionally
look at the results.
—Winston Churchill

## Effectiveness Is Not an Afterthought

During the first stage of the AXLES model, the focus was on defining success for the mentoring program. A critical component to an effective and sustainable program is designing a mentoring experience that aligns to key measures of success.

As you continue working through the model, make sure to continually check in and align the program to best accomplish your predefined outcomes. Each decision you make in the Design the Experience and Program Launch stages should be with the mentoring program purpose statement in mind.

Remember, not achieving goals is not the only way a mentoring program can fail. In reality, many of these programs never had a documented goal to achieve in the first place. Many well-intentioned programs are designed with poorly defined guidance, such as "People should like the program." But that isn't a goal, and it's definitely not aligned to a specific talent need.

Even worse are those programs that begin with designs instead of purpose. For example, when program leaders define success as a "six-month, formal, one-on-one program," which is a program format. If you build a program that lasts six months and involves a traditional structure, will the program be successful? No! That sort of guidance does not help you understand how to measure the impact of the program on your organization's most critical talent needs.

Fortunately, during the Align to a Purpose stage (chapter 2) you defined the success of your program. Then, as you continued to move through the model, you refined those strategic outcomes. This is so important because you cannot effectively measure the impact of the program after it is over. Evaluating results is a through-line of the development process for all talent development solutions, especially mentoring programs.

While the AXLES model simplifies the development approach for formal mentoring programs, there is considerable flexibility in the design process. In the real world, all the planning for evaluating effectiveness should be done while you're designing the experience, planning the program launch, and generating participant support. The execution work in reviewing the mentoring program effectiveness is an ongoing process, starting before the program is launched and continuing through the program's life cycle.

## Tell a Story of Success

As a practice, evaluating effectiveness is not about one-time measurements and hitting a magic number. The success of a mentoring program lies in the ongoing mentoring relationships and experiences, which should generate feedback on the program over time. This feedback, and data gathered from different aspects of the program, serves to create a narrative about the program's impact on the organization.

For example, let's say you started out in the Align to a Purpose stage with a success measure of increasing employee retention by 10 percent. Conventional methods would suggest that you look at your retention numbers about 12 months after a mentoring program launch. If the number went up by 11 percent, the program was successful. Right? Wrong!

In that example, there's such a large gap in the information on hand that it's impossible to tell what happened. There is nothing to indicate what happened during or immediately after the program to improve behaviors that would lead to an increase in retention. Maybe the program was amazingly effective, and learners improved critical skill sets for retaining talent on their teams. Or maybe the program was a total bust, but there happened to be a concurrent diversity and inclusion initiative that rallied employee loyalty, which was actually responsible for the increase in retention. Or maybe the reality was somewhere in between: The program was mediocre and others factors influenced the retention numbers. Without a more complete picture, you can have no idea what influence your mentoring program has on retention, and you certainly can't claim any success.

The easy path is to accept that retention went up and assume that the mentoring program was a key contributing factor. However, not only is that a flawed approach, it's quite risky. Let's turn that example around. What if the retention numbers went down? By the same conventional logic, the mentoring program must have been such a horrific disaster that it caused a mass exodus of employees from the organization—the exact opposite outcome you had hoped for. Again, consider what you don't know. It's likely that the program was not at fault, but that some other environmental factor, such as a change in compensation structure or work policy, played a part in the increase in turnover. Another possibility is that the program was very well designed to increase retention, but wasn't scaled to make a big enough impact.

Without information about what happens between the program launch and the strategic results, you have to fill in the blanks with assumptions, which do not usually work in the mentoring program's favor.

Your job is to design an evaluation that provides a clear and complete narrative of the program's impact on participants and the organization. You want to tell a story of success: How did the program lead to personal and professional development, which in turn influenced job performance, and finally achieved results at a strategic level?

## Using the New World Kirkpatrick Model to Evaluate Results

To determine your program's success, we turn to the road-tested Kirkpatrick Model of Evaluation, originally developed by Donald L. Kirkpatrick more than six decades ago. This process for evaluating results is continuing to drive measurement in the talent management industry through the ongoing work of Jim and Wendy Kirkpatrick.

There are other models and processes that can be used to evaluate the effectiveness of talent development solutions (including mentoring programs), but this is the most intuitive and easy to apply. The Kirkpatrick model is focused on achieving results and getting return on effort, which is exactly what leaders are most concerned with. However, the most important consideration is that you use a proven process for evaluating effectiveness, even if it's not the one described in this chapter.

The New World Kirkpatrick Model—a newly redesigned approach to the Kirkpatrick model, developed by Jim and Wendy Kirkpatrick in 2015—focuses on crafting a story about results through multiple levels of gathering data and feedback. This approach emphasizes the need to build the story over time, rather than a single point in time. Because mentoring is a sustained relationship-driven learning process, simply collecting data at a single point in time does not provide enough information to get a complete picture of effectiveness.

This model also advocates measuring leading indicators rather than lagging indicators. A leading indicator, for example, might be a quick learner survey to rate mentor engagement levels each month. This helps us determine whether learners think their mentors are engaged, and allows us to address any issues that come up proactively. Conversely, a lagging indicator might be asking that same question, but at the end of a 12-month program when we don't have a chance to use the information to improve the program experience.

Table 5-1 provides a brief summary of how the Kirkpatrick model can be applied in a mentoring program situation. For more information, check out Jim and Wendy Kirkpatrick's book, *Kirkpatrick's Four Levels of Evaluation*.

## Table 5-1. Evaluation Overview

| Level | Description | Example Sources | Application to Mentoring Programs |
|---|---|---|---|
| Level 1: Reaction | Measures learner satisfaction, engagement, and relevance of content to learner's job | • Interviews<br>• Focus groups<br>• Surveys<br>• Anecdotes<br>• Assessments | Because of the unique learning environment, Level 1 data should be gathered frequently and from various sources |
| Level 2: Learning | Measures how well learners have gained knowledge, skills, attitude, confidence, and commitment | • 360-degree assessments<br>• Observations<br>• Mentor evaluations<br>• Role plays<br>• Action plans | Assessing learning in mentoring programs should include learner-driven measures, as well as measures from the mentor or supervisor |
| Level 3: Behavior | Measures how well the learner is able to use the new knowledge on the job, and includes an assessment of systems and processes that influence performance | • 360-degree assessments<br>• Observations<br>• Performance reviews<br>• Supervisor evaluations<br>• Action plan reviews<br>• Individual development plans | Job performance often begins improving during the formal mentoring process, and should start to be assessed before the end of the program |
| Level 4: Results | Measures the effect on target success measures, includes leading indicators, which are short-term observations that indicate the learner is on track to improve | • Mentoring program purpose statement<br>• Strategic key performance indicators | What you measure for Level 4 should be easy to answer—look to your work in step 1 of the AXLES model |

Adapted from The New World Kirkpatrick Model.

## Planning Top Down

To create a complete story of success for your mentoring program, plan the evaluation process starting with Level 4 and then work down through the model to Level 1.

Remember that the Evaluate Effectiveness phase should be at least partially finished at the very beginning of the project. Determining what Level 4 success looks like after developing your mentoring program will not lead to success—the best way to ensure alignment and create substantial strategic impact is to define success early, and design the experience to meet those goals. Here's a story to illustrate this idea:

> Once, when my daughter was 4 years old, I walked into our kitchen to find everything from the lower shelves of the pantry and refrigerator on the countertop. She had our largest mixing bowl filled with cereal, raisins, uncooked spaghetti, string cheese, and even whole peaches. Equal parts intrigued and irritated, I asked her, "What are you making?" She looked down at her bowl and said, "I don't know yet. I'll tell you when it's cooked."

That's what happens when we don't define success at the beginning and use it to guide our decisions! We end up with a concoction that isn't going to work for anyone.

By the way, that isn't where the story ends. When my daughter's aimless experimenting didn't work out the way she hoped, guess who had to clean up the mess? Me! As practitioners, if we do not continue to act as trusted consultative partners who push for what's needed for our mentoring program to succeed, the failure of the program will come back to haunt us one way or another.

By starting your planning with Level 4: Results, you keep your program's strategic purpose front and center. Ask yourself, "How do I measure success?" You already answered part of this question at the beginning of the development process in the Align to a Purpose step, when you defined the organization's vision of strategic success. However, throughout the development process you may have continued refining your definition of success. Read through your program purpose statement from the Align to a Purpose component will to help define how to measure success.

Table 5-2 provides some examples of Level 4 metrics for measuring both quantitative and qualitative data.

## Table 5-2. Planning Evaluation

| Purpose | Quantitative Data | Qualitative Data |
| --- | --- | --- |
| Increase employee engagement | Employee engagement survey results | Office culture |
| Increase retention of key talent | Retention statistics | Personal stories of transformation |
| Increase diversity and inclusion | Hiring and promotion diversity numbers | Anecdotes of increased inclusion |
| Improve talent pipeline for critical positions | Internal candidate pipeline and time to success in key roles | Leadership rates candidates "ready now" |
| Increase profitability | Revenue and P&L | Employee confidence and productivity |

When you choose the metrics to capture your program's intended outcomes, it's best to select items that are already being measured by the organization. For example, what if success was defined as "increased employee engagement" during the Align step, and then refined to "employee engagement scores in every division average 80 percent or higher" during program development. That's great! But, how do you measure the outcomes? If your company does a biannual engagement survey, it will gather and track the data you need. On the other hand, if the organization doesn't have anything in place to track engagement, you either have to choose another metric or build in a significant increase in project scope and effort.

When looking at Level 4 measures, it's important to remember that strategic measures are sometimes slower to implement than tactical ones. Discuss with your project sponsor and stakeholders a reasonable timeline for seeing impact on your Level 4 measures. It might be a big perspective shift for them to think about seeing Level 4 results improve over time rather than looking for a single point of success. Remember, mentoring relationships are key to sustainable performance improvement, which leads to lasting organizational change.

## Connecting Strategic Results and Performance

As you continue to plan your approach to evaluating your mentoring program, you should take a look at how to measure Level 3: Behavior. Depending on design of the mentoring program, and the effectiveness of your mentors, performance improvement can begin soon after the launch of the program, so your plan should involve multiple points of review. Consider evaluating Level 3 toward the end of the formal program, soon after the cycle is concluded, and then again three months later. However, the best times to measure your program will vary.

To assess behavior, connect your Level 4 measures to Level 3 by asking the question, "What are the learner performance factors and behaviors that will ultimately lead to Level 4 success?" Table 5-3 has some examples of connecting Level 4 to Level 3.

## From Behavior to Learning

The next step is to identify the measures that are best for evaluating Level 2: Learning. As with the other levels, you should approach this by asking, "What learning (or development) leads to learners demonstrating the Level 3 behaviors needed for success?"

In traditional face-to-face or virtual training, learning is relatively easy to measure. After all, you brought everyone together to learn specific new skills or knowledge, so just measure whether that happened. However, in mentoring programs this is less clear because learning is much more individualized. To assess how well a learner's development is progressing, consider using some of the tools outlined in Table 5-4. (By the way, these tools can also be used to measure Level 3.)

## Table 5-3. Level 4 to Level 3 Example

| Defined Program Success | Level 4 Measures | Level 3 Measures |
|---|---|---|
| Employee engagement above x% | Employee engagement scores | • Productivity (and effectiveness)<br>• Discretionary effort<br>• Fewer days off<br>• Use of online communities |
| Sufficient leadership pipeline for expected openings | Number of internal promotions vs. external hires<br><br>Identified group of mobile high potentials | • 9-box assessments<br>• Performance reviews<br>• Internal applications<br>• Interview results |
| Improve junior employee retention through improved onboarding | 3-month, 6-month, and 12-month retention numbers for employees<br><br>Exit and stay interviews | • Performance observation<br>• Qualitative learner feedback (cultural fit)<br>• Team feedback<br>• Career development planning |

## Table 5-4. Level 3 to Level 2 Example

| Tool | Level 2 Measures | A Word of Caution |
|---|---|---|
| Individual Development Plans (IDPs) | A well-crafted IDP is a great way to measure ongoing learner progress. These serve as a common reference guide for learners, mentors, supervisors, and program administrators. IDPs are most powerful when used in mentoring programs in which learning goals vary widely between learners. | Avoid using IDPs if you cannot provide guidance to participants on best practices for creating them. In these cases, IDPs become a compliance exercise and do not reflect learner progress. |
| 360-Degree Assessments | 360-degree assessments show trending performance change among learners. They can be done before the program begins, periodically during the program (every 6 months), and then again at the end of the program cycle to capture data on job skills or competencies. | Avoid 360-degree assessments with a large population of learners, or if you plan to scale the program up. These assessments require more effort from program administrators, which goes up with the number of learners. |
| Role-Play Observation Forms | Having prescribed role play between a learner and mentor is a great way to assess improvement. The mentor's observations of the learner's performance provides valuable data in aggregate. Like other tools, these can be implemented at regular intervals during the mentoring program. | Because role-play observation forms can be generic or tailored to several situations, this is a very adaptable Level 2 tool. The only word of caution is that mentors may require some training on how to best facilitate role play. |

## Satisfaction, Engagement, and Relevance

Planning to evaluate the effectiveness of the mentoring program continues by choosing how to get Level 1 feedback on learner satisfaction, engagement, and the relevance of mentorship content to the job. Practitioners commonly measure Level 1: Reaction with "smile sheets," or simple surveys given at the end of a learning event. However, because a mentoring program is an extended experience, you should measure Level 1 at several points during the process.

As a general guideline for larger extended programs, you should take some form of measurement at least once every three months. In many cases, it is more effective to gather feedback more regularly, such monthly.

One way to get frequent feedback without overwhelming participants with surveys is to vary both the audience and the method of data collection. For example, you could alternate between surveying learners one month and interviewing mentors the next. Or, you could conduct monthly focus group conference calls, inviting different participants each month.

So, what do you measure in Level 1? Effective feedback provides information and opinions about how satisfied the learners and mentors are with the process and form of the mentoring program, their mentoring relationships, and their own progress. In addition, Level 1 data should also paint a picture of how engaged and motivated the learners and mentors are in their work. Finally, you will also want to discover how relevant the mentoring conversations (and provided content, if applicable) are to the learners' work from their perspective.

Level 1 is all about learner and mentor perceptions. For example, let's say you and the project sponsor decided that every mentoring conversation this month should include a discussion on the dress code policy. However, after the month is over, some learners still think the policy isn't relevant or important to their work. Because they don't understand why the policy is relevant, it will continue to negatively affect their experience, which will be reflected in their Level 1 evaluations. (By the way, the easiest and quickest way to address this conflict of need to know versus want to know is to make sure you explain the WIIFM or "what's in it for me" for learners)

It doesn't matter how you collect feedback and information on participant satisfaction, engagement, and relevance, as long as the questions are framed in learner-centered language. This helps learners identify more closely with the questions and reflect more accurately on their experience. Table 5-5 presents some typical program-centered Level 1 survey items and how to reframe them as learner-centered.

## Table 5-5. Level 1 Program-Centered and Learner-Centered Survey Items

| Level 1 Factors | Program-Centered Survey Items | Learner-Centered Survey Items |
|---|---|---|
| Satisfaction | Feedback provided by mentor is helpful. | My mentor provides helpful feedback. |
| Satisfaction | Mentoring relationship has resulted in access to people or resources. | My mentor has introduced me to new people or resources. |
| Engagement | Who is primarily leading the goal-setting conversations in the mentoring relationship? | I am actively involved in or lead goal-setting conversations for my mentoring relationship. |
| Engagement | Who is primarily responsible for creating mentor meeting agendas? | I contribute to the structure and agendas for meetings in my mentor relationship. |
| Relevance | Available mentoring resources are valuable for the participant. | I find the resources available for the mentoring program valuable. |
| Relevance | Skills and knowledge acquired through mentoring are relevant to participant on the job. | I am improving skills that are useful in my work through this mentoring program. |

Remember, you are also going to want to involve your mentors in evaluating Level 1. The same rules apply for making sure your questions are framed in a way that allows participants (learners and mentors) to be in control.

Now that you have successfully worked through each of the four levels and determined the best approaches for measuring the effectiveness of your program, you need to put everything together into one cohesive evaluation plan. A template is available in appendix D to help you.

## From Information to Insights

Now that you have a plan for tracking the data, what do you do with them? Most important, have you set aside an appropriate amount of time to review and analyze the incoming feedback?

One of the most undermining evaluation practices is putting effort into surveys and other evaluation tools, only to omit the data from your analysis. Unused data are a monumental waste of time for those who designed the tools and implemented the evaluation, as well as the participants who took the time to give their feedback. And of course, data that haven't been analyzed do not help improve the program or tell the story of effectiveness.

❂ The goal in reviewing data is to gain insights from the information—across all four levels of evaluation, look for trends, outlying comments, innovative suggestions, and early indicators of program performance.

Some high-level views of interpreting data are captured in Tables 5-6 and 5-7, which address trends that might appear at different levels, and how they can start to come together to tell a story. Each table compares positive or negative results from one level of evaluation with positive or negative results from another level of evaluation. The idea is to look at how these results combine to tell a story of success, or even help diagnose potential issues.

## Table 5-6. Comparison of Level 1 and Level 2 Data

| | Level 1 Data Show Positive Results | Level 1 Data Show Negative Results |
|---|---|---|
| **Level 2 Data Show Positive Results** | Level 1 data show that learners and mentors are happy with the program, engaged, and see the relevance of what they're doing. Level 2 data show progress in learning goals.<br><br>**Result:** Program is aligned and on track! | Level 1 data show that learners and mentors aren't fully satisfied with the program, but Level 2 data show learning is progressing.<br><br>**Result:** Improve program processes and communication. Involve learner and mentor stakeholders. |
| **Level 2 Data Show Negative Results** | Level 1 data show that learners and mentors are engaged and satisfied, but learning data are not showing success.<br><br>**Result:** Implement additional participant support for mentoring relationships. Check alignment between the design and program purpose statement. | Learners and mentors are unhappy with the program and learning progress is not taking place.<br><br>**Result:** Start with focus groups of learners and mentors to check process support and program alignment to the purpose statement. A poor experience with the program is likely undermining the learning potential. |

## Table 5-7. Comparison of Level 2 and Level 3 Data

| | Level 3 Data Show Positive Results | Level 3 Data Show Negative Results |
|---|---|---|
| **Level 2 Data Show Positive Results** | Level 2 data show that learners are making progress during their mentoring relationships, which is transferring to performance improvement on the job.<br><br>**Result:** Program is aligned and on track! | Learners seem to be doing well with Level 2 learning, but are not transferring improved skills to the job.<br><br>**Result:** Investigate factors external to the program, such as supervisor support, technology, or process barriers to learning transfer. |
| **Level 2 Data Show Negative Results** | Learners are improving their performance, but Level 2 data show the improvement isn't due to mentoring. Why?<br><br>**Result:** Check Level 2 measurement tools. Are these valid for measuring learning in mentoring relationships? Then, talk to stakeholders about other factors that might be contributing to Level 3 success. Can you combine those efforts with the mentoring program to get greater results? | Mentoring relationships don't seem to be resulting in development growth in the learning environment or transfer back to the job.<br><br>**Result:** Start with focus groups of learners and mentors to check whether the content of the program is aligned and mentors are receiving enough support to achieve success. Make small adjustments until you start to see success; don't go for a total overhaul! |

It is important to keep in mind that terms such as positive results and negative results are intentionally generic. Each program, and especially each set of evaluation practices, will be different in what you consider positive or negative results. For example, the benchmark for positive Level 1 results for one program might be higher or lower than what is considered positive for another program.

## Iterative Improvement

The insights you gain over time from evaluating the effectiveness of your mentoring program serve two related purposes. First, they inform stakeholders of how well the program is achieving intended results (defined in the first step of the model). Second, those insights and feedback become the basis for improving the program iteratively.

Publish the program's feedback and evaluation results publicly whenever possible. This transparency shows stakeholders and participants your serious intent to continue improving the program to create the best possible experience. It also demonstrates that the efforts that participants have made in responding to surveys, participating in focus groups, and so forth is well spent, because they can see that the data are actively being used. This transparency also encourages participants to invest more fully and authentically in the evaluation process.

However, it isn't always appropriate to make results available. It also is usually best to share the insights gained from data, rather than the whole of the data set. Sharing that story of success and the identified needs for improvement is usually more effective in reaching participants. Sharing the actual data sets can also lead to privacy issues, where participants are worried about specific concerns being linked back to them. In addition, it can be really effective to share what actions the evaluation has led to, such as program improvements or scaling the program to include more participants.

The next step is to determine which (if any) improvements should be made to better accomplish the program's purpose. You should implement an iterative, or stepped, approach to improving your mentoring program, prioritizing improvements by expected return on effort. Those items that are likely to get you much closer to the results you want with relatively little effort should be the first to get implemented. Of course, if you discover that aspects of the program are detrimental to participants, fix those right away.

Be sure to consider how program changes will affect participant experience—too much shifting in program structure, procedures, or timelines can be overwhelming for learners and mentors who are in the middle of a program cycle, especially if that type of change keeps happening. Too much change at once can also have the unintended consequence of making the program feel unfinished, not credible, or not valuable. An iterative, transparent approach, where evaluation results are leveraged to identify the most important incremental changes, is the best way to improve the program.

The final argument for slow, but valuable, updates to your program is that many Level 4 results might not be fully realized in a short timeframe. If the program undergoes several major changes over the course of the year, it may be hard to determine which changes positively affected the program's accomplishments and which were working against them.

## Risk Management

Every mentoring program, and really every talent development solution, comes with risks to the outcomes of the program. There are situations where, no matter how diligently you follow the AXLES model, potential obstacles still need to be proactively addressed. Some challenges may not need immediate action, but should still be taken into consideration so that a plan is ready to address them if they do surface.

### Risk 1: Learners Repeatedly Fail to Meet Outcomes

There are times when learners continue to fail to meet certain Level 2 or Level 3 benchmarks, despite an aligned program that has been designed to be the best possible experience. In these situations, look first to evaluation data to determine if there are process or program structure changes that can address the gap. Following those changes, do some discovery work around the learners' environment to find out if factors external to the mentoring program are negatively influencing the results. Examples include supervisor support of new behavior, fear of reactions from colleagues, conflicting job expectations or policies, or even a lack of access to needed resources or technology. In a situation where external factors are reducing impact of the mentoring program, consider additional nontraining solutions, such as supervisor playbooks, corporate communication blitzes, or even policy changes.

### Risk 2: Mentors Fail to Deliver, Show Up, or Engage

If practitioners do not have the option of choosing the mentors for their program, which is often the case, the risk increases of having mentors who are not effective. This could be because the mentors do not have the skill sets, are too busy and don't show up, or just simply don't put in the effort necessary to make the mentoring relationships work.

The first step is to proactively address this risk by giving the mentors as much skill development and support as possible leading up to and during the program. Make sure they are empowered with knowledge of the program's purpose (what you are trying to achieve together) and resources that will help them mentor efficiently and effectively. (We'll discuss this further in chapter 6.)

If you think your program is at risk, another proactive tactic is to discuss this risk with your project sponsor early in the design process. Together, plan how you'll address disengaged or ineffective mentors, who will be responsible for dealing with them, and ultimately whether or not mentors can be removed from the program. (See chapter 3 for more about this.)

There are also a few steps you can take during the program, if evaluation results show that mentors are not helping the learner experience the way they should, including:

- Engage with a senior leader or your project sponsor to individually address mentors with poor evaluation results.
- Create an informal mentor community that all mentors in the program can use to help one another develop.
- Ask top performing mentors to build a formal mentoring relationship with underperforming mentors (meta-mentoring).
- Have a program administrator observe underperforming mentors during a mentoring meeting (with permission) to provide just-in-time coaching.
- When all else fails, ask mentors to take a break from the program until they are able to engage with more effort.

## Risk 3: Leaders Fail to Support the Program

Few things undermine the success of a program as much as when those in leadership positions do not support mentoring, or worse, speak publicly against it. In most of these situations, the problem isn't necessarily the program design. More often, it's because the leaders are irritated that their expertise and opinions were not considered during the development of the program.

This is why you should spend time talking to stakeholders and getting input during the Align to a Purpose phase. This helps to proactively build champions for the program and increase stakeholder buy-in.

If that doesn't work, and some leaders are still resisting the mentoring program, set up a meeting with each individual to get feedback. The effort you should put into gathering their feedback and acting on it depends on their role, as well as how much influence they have in your program's success. This statement usually helps leaders feel like they have been heard, but does not create too much commitment: "Thank you very much for sharing your concerns and thoughts. Your input is valuable to the process, and I don't think the program can fully achieve success without you behind it. I will share your thoughts with the team and we will reach out to you soon to let you know what we think we can do."

However, make sure you put some action behind this statement—be prepared to follow through, and hopefully, you'll be able to turn your critic into a champion for the mentoring program.

## Risk 4: The Orignial Most Critical Talent Issues Change

Sometimes an organization's most pressing talent needs evolve after the program has been launched. While it might seem like a catastrophe at first, this doesn't have to mean the program failed. Fixing the issue will take significant effort, but the bulk of that work will likely be invisible to participants and won't affect their experience too much.

For example, consider a traditional calendar-based program that was designed to help develop high-potential leaders so they were ready for critical roles. The organization's most senior leaders defined this goal as critical because the company was growing at a fast pace and needed more middle managers to be ready to fill newly created senior positions. Then let's say that something happens that affects the organization economically, and the anticipated growth stalls out before the program can launch. Now the most critical need is to have middle managers who can help their teams pull through a tough period. You will need to rework the decisions you made during the Align to a Purpose stage and other components to reconfigure the focus of the program. However, the audience and some of the design decisions will remain the same.

In general, if a change in organizational priorities occurs, the best thing to do is go back to the Align to a Purpose step of the AXLES model. This might take some work initially, but you may find that much of your program design can stay the same.

---

# Using the New World Kirkpatrick Model for Mentoring

Jim and Wendy Kirkpatrick, Co-Founders, Kirkpatrick Partners

Training budgets are among the first to be cut when economic times get tough, which means that training programs need to prove their value now more than ever. You can use the New World Kirkpatrick Model to demonstrate the organizational value of your work by creating an effective training evaluation plan for any program.

The New World Kirkpatrick Model uses the four levels of evaluation and adds new elements to help people operationalize it effectively. It begins with Level 4.

## Level 4

Clarity regarding the true Level 4: Results of an organization is critical. By definition, it is some combination of the organizational purpose and mission (Figure 5-1).

**Figure 5-1. Level 4 Result**

Every organization has just one Level 4 result. However, many find it hard relate a single training class to a high-level organizational mission because business results are broad and long term. Based on the efforts of people, departments, and environmental factors, results can take months or years to manifest. This is where leading indicators come into play.

Leading indicators help bridge the gap between individual initiatives and efforts, and organizational results. These short-term observations and measurements suggest that critical behaviors are on track to create a positive impact on the desired results. Common leading indicators include customer satisfaction, employee engagement, sales volume, and market share.

## Level 3

Level 3 is the degree to which participants apply what they learned during training when they are back on the job (Figure 5-2). The New World Level 3: Behavior consists of critical behaviors, required drivers, and on-the-job learning.

Critical behaviors are specific actions that have the biggest impact on the desired results if they are performed consistently on the job. An employee may perform thousands of behaviors on the job, but critical behaviors are those that are the most important to achieving organizational success.

The New World Kirkpatrick Model also adds required drivers—processes and systems that reinforce, monitor, encourage, and reward performance of critical behaviors on the job—to Level 3. Think of them as the lights, signs, and guardrails on a bridge: They show the right path and are there to keep people on track if they start to go astray. Required drivers decrease the likelihood of people falling through the cracks, or deliberately crawling through the cracks if they are not interested in performing the required behaviors. Examples of required drivers include job aids, refreshers (on demand or scheduled), coaching, mentoring, recognition and rewards for demonstrating the right behaviors, and interviews and focus groups to discuss on-the-job performance.

A strong Level 3 plan, including clearly defined critical behaviors and a thoughtfully selected group of required drivers, is one of the biggest factors for program success and ultimate accomplishment of high-level goals.

### Figure 5-2. Level 3 Measures

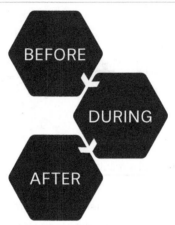

When Level 3 critical behaviors and required drivers are defined during the training design process, it's easy to build them into participants' training and pretraining communication. This has a number of benefits for training participants:

- increased engagement during the session
- lower anxiety surrounding new processes or information
- higher degree of self-responsibility
- increased confidence and commitment to apply the new information.

Most important, the table is set for training participants to succeed when they return to their jobs.

Creating a cultural expectation that individuals are responsible for maintaining the knowledge and skills to enhance their own performance will encourage them to be accountable and feel empowered. That is why on-the-job learning was added to the New World Level 3. It provides an opportunity for employees and their employers to share the responsibility for good performance.

## Level 2

The original definition of Level 2: Learning is the degree to which participants acquire the intended knowledge, skills, and attitudes based on their participation in the learning event. Confidence and commitment were added to Level 2 in the New World Kirkpatrick Model to help close the gap between learning and behavior, and prevent the cycle of waste when training is repeated for people who possess the required knowledge and skills but fail to perform appropriately on the job.

Confidence is defined as the degree to which training participants think they will be able to do what they learned during training on the job. Addressing confidence during training brings learners closer to the desired on-the-job performance. Commitment is defined as the degree to which learners intend to apply the knowledge and skills learned during training to their jobs. It relates to learner motivation by acknowledging that even if the knowledge and skills are mastered, effort still must be put forth to use the information or perform the skills on a daily basis.

# Level 1

Level 1: Reaction is the degree to which participants react favorably to the learning event. The New World Kirkpatrick Level 1: Reaction has three dimensions: customer satisfaction, relevance, and engagement.

Customer satisfaction relates to participants' level of satisfaction with the training. Relevance is the degree to which training participants have the opportunity to use or apply what they learned. It is important because even the best training is a waste of resources if the participants have no application for the content in their everyday work. Engagement refers to the degree to which participants are actively involved in and contributing to the learning experience. Engagement levels directly relate to the level of learning that is attained.

Learning and development professionals enter new territory in the New World Kirkpatrick Model (Figure 5-3), expanding their role to that of learning and performance consultants. This may require some courage and a bit of adjustment, but if you embrace this new worldview, you can become an indispensable partner to the business you serve.

## Figure 5-3. The New World Kirkpatrick Model

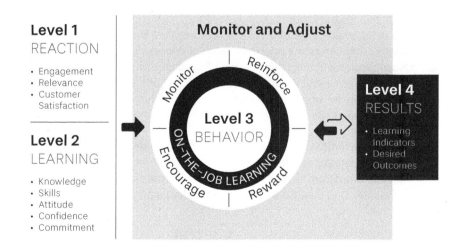

# Conclusion

Evaluating the effectiveness of your mentoring program is no less critical than any other stage of development. Even though effectiveness is the fourth step in the AXLES model, success was designed from the very beginning, leading to more clarity in determining how well the program is meeting its goals.

Mentoring programs are not single events; they're relationships that are built over time. Likewise, evaluating effectiveness is not a one-time effort; it's a process that is ongoing, allowing for incremental course corrections.

Through use of the four levels of evaluation, you can build a story of success for your program. Use it to show your stakeholders a complete picture of how the mentoring program is providing relevant and engaging learning experiences for participants, which translate to increased performance on the job and ultimately greater strategic results.

Proactively planning how to measure each level of evaluation is a straightforward process of working backwards from Level 4 to Level 3, Level 2, and Level 1 to create a cohesive narration about the effect of mentoring on the organization.

### Key Insights: Evaluating for Results

1. Begin defining success during the Align to a Purpose phase and continue to refine the definition throughout the process.
2. Point-in-time measures are incomplete. Plan to review results of the program regularly to check in and see impact over time.
3. Use the New World Kirkpatrick Model of Evaluation to plan what information to gather to measure the effectiveness of your mentoring program.
4. Measuring all four levels—results, behavior, learning, and reaction—is the key to telling your program's success story.
5. Define the strategic results (Level 4) that translate to success for the program and determine how to measure those results.
6. Use measurement tools that are already available or easy to implement.
7. Be transparent about program feedback and results, as well as how the feedback will (or won't) influence change in the mentoring program.
8. Use an iterative approach to improve your mentoring program over time without major disruption to participants.
9. Use leading indicators to help bridge the gap between individual efforts and organizational results.
10. Plan backward from Level 4 to Level 1, and use the sample evaluation plan in appendix D to create a thorough and cohesive process for reviewing your mentoring program for effectiveness.

# Chapter Exercises

## Perception Change

Lead a discussion with your project sponsor and stakeholders about measuring the effectiveness of your mentoring program before it is launched (preferably during the design phase). Use the following questions as a guide:

- What is the definition of success from the Align phase? How should it be refined?
- How can you measure success? What metrics and tools are available?
- Over what period should you expect Level 4 strategic measures to reasonably change? How often should you review results?
- If Level 4 strategic results show no improvement after while, what course of action will you take to investigate? What if there are external factors influencing the results?
- If you see positive progress on your Level 4 strategic results, how would build on that momentum? Will you scale the program to a larger audience?

## Mentoring Program Evaluation Plan

Craft a plan for a sustained, regular review of program effectiveness. The goal is to develop a process that gathers data and feedback over time to create a story of impact about the mentoring program. Use the template in appendix D to help you.

# 6
# Support Participants

> The delicate balance of mentoring someone is not
> creating them in your own image, but giving them the
> opportunity to create themselves.
> —Steven Spielberg

## Support the Experience

Mentoring is a process—your mentoring program is essentially an extended learning experience. In the Design the Experience step of the AXLES model, you devoted a lot of time to thinking about how the program's structure, schedule, and matching processes affect the participant experience. You also defined how learners and mentors can enter and exit the program, as well as what is expected of them while in the program.

During the Support Participants step of the AXLES model, you'll continue that work, investing in the support structure necessary for the learners and mentors to succeed. The goal is to support the participant experience through mentor preparation, communication, materials, program administration, and creating a community.

After the program launches, learners and mentors enter into a low-visibility period, during which they build relationships, set goals, and establish trust outside the view of program administrators. Depending on the formality and complexity of the program's design, program administrators and participants may not have significant, planned interactions for a while after the program launches. Informal programs that have been designed with less structure will have even fewer planned touch points.

During this step, you want to make sure that even though all the activity is occurring outside the visibility of the learning function, mentors and learners feel supported in every way. They should have the information, resources, and tools they need to be successful; if they have any questions or concerns, they should know where to go for answers. This chapter outlines several methods you can use to provide important support resources for participants in your mentoring program.

# Mentor Skills Development

The first step in supporting participants is to prepare program mentors as well as possible for the role they are taking on. Whether your mentors are going to be in one-on-one relationships or leading mentoring groups, they will likely still need to develop several skills—active listening, questioning, diagnosis, performance support, and effectively giving direction—to be effective.

Increasing the effectiveness of your mentor pool through development is one of the most effective ways you can spend project time and financial resources, because skilled mentors are key to the mentoring program's success. Even if your program is aligned and well designed, it will accomplish nothing with ineffective mentors. Learners can only reach their goals if they have a positive mentoring experience—if their learning goals are not met, job performance will not improve, and the program's strategic goals will not be met. A lot depends on mentor effectiveness.

As mentioned in the previous chapter, most mentors, even mentors who are already very good, are grateful for any help they receive in developing their mentoring skill set. There are those mentors who believe they have nothing new to learn, but they are the exception and usually change their tune after being offered development opportunities.

When you offer these development opportunities depends on your program structure, schedule, and the mentor population. In general, if you know who will be part of the mentor pool before the program launches, it's best to offer resources before the kickoff meeting. But regardless of your program's design, you should invest in mentor skills development on an ongoing basis throughout the program cycle.

The following ideas for mentor skills development are a starting point for designing a comprehensive support system for your mentors. Some ideas will work better than others, depending on your organizational culture, mentor availability, and the program design. You can also take one of these basic ideas and shape it to fit your situation.

## Prelaunch Events

If your mentor population is defined before the mentoring program launches, it is helpful to bring them together virtually or face-to-face to share key information about the program. During these events, focus on providing information about being an effective mentor, clarifying any concerns, sharing contact information in case of further questions, and above all else, thanking the mentors for their participation.

One format that works well for these prelaunch events is a two-hour webinar with a preset agenda. Share the agenda before the webinar and ask mentors to send in any questions ahead of time so you can prepare responses. Make sure to record the webinars and post them online for mentors to review if they could not attend. If you have a large group of mentor participants, consider holding more than one webinar to accommodate different schedules.

## Virtual Role Plays

Using web conferencing software or teleconferencing, create small mentor group events before and during the program cycle. Use these events for mentors to challenge themselves with assigned role-play scenarios, particularly around difficult situations that might arise while mentoring. For example, have mentors talk through a situation in which a learner shares being unhappy with the way her supervisor talks to her. Role play is an effective way to develop someone's comfort level with uncomfortable conversations, or to practice skills such as active listening and questioning. Role play won't work in every organization's culture, but if it is right for your program, use it. Mentors don't want to feel unprepared for their mentoring conversations, and many worry that they will be caught off guard without having the answers they need. Role-play activities, followed by peer feedback, are a great way to help mentors feel more prepared and confident.

Try creating a monthly theme, such as career development or difficult conversations, and send out three role-play scenarios corresponding to that theme. This way, when participants attend the webinar, they will be more prepared.

## Monthly Skills Focus

Organize support resources by identifying a skills focus (or target competency) each month, which you can then support using a variety of tools, readings, role-play exercises, or live events. If your program includes work on individual development plans (IDPs), 9-box assessments, or any other kind of competency or skill-based list, it's easy to find out which specific areas are in most need of support and focus.

## Mentor Highlights

Mentoring is all about learning from others, so why not share a successful mentor story to help excite participants about their own mentoring relationships? Each month or quarter, select a mentor with outstanding evaluation results, and interview him about his approach to mentoring. Ask him to share questions he likes to ask to challenge learners and developmental assignments he uses. Publish the "Mentor Superstar" column in an email blast or on the program's intranet site so that other mentors can benefit.

## Readings and Assignments

Sometimes mentors are just too busy to sign in to a scheduled web conference or participate in events. Assigned readings and activities are a more self-paced method for providing skill development resources to your mentors.

Articles from online journals and magazines related to your organization's industry are a great way to encourage mentors in their self-development. Most industries have trade publications that include articles about talent issues. Other great resources include *Harvard Business Review*, *TD* magazine, and publications by the Center for Creative Leadership.

Don't be shy about giving mentors practice development activities. For example, ask them to, "Use your active listening skills in a meeting with a direct report this week. Take notes on how it improved meeting communication and any aspects of active listening that you would like to practice further."

These assignments are usually optional, but may be just what the mentor needs. They are quick ways to grow skills without considerable effort. Even if a mentor chooses not to complete the assignment, the prompt itself might be a good way to keep development skills on her radar.

## Mentor Expectations

One resource that mentors appreciate is documentation explaining what it means to be a good mentor, and expectations of the role. Creating a table of effective and ineffective mentor behaviors can be very helpful to mentors who are learning how to be more effective. Table 6-1 provides a list of effective and ineffective mentor behaviors, which you can adapt to fit your organization.

### Table 6-1. Effective and Ineffective Mentor Behavior

| Effective Mentor Behavior | Ineffective Mentor Behavior |
| --- | --- |
| • Facilitates problem solving<br>• Listens effectively<br>• Supports<br>• Gives timely feedback<br>• Provides some direction<br>• Makes suggestions<br>• Helps the learner understand cultural context<br>• Connects with resources<br>• Seeks to develop<br>• Challenges<br>• Acts as catalyst<br>• Boosts confidence<br>• Recognizes progress | • Fixes problems<br>• Assumes responsibility for learner's problems<br>• Overprotective<br>• Gives overly critical feedback<br>• Only uses direction<br>• Acts as though there is only one "right way"<br>• Avoids difficult development work<br>• Insensitive to learner needs<br>• Shelters learner from obstacles<br>• Discounts learner's feelings<br>• Overly complimentary<br>• Lacks follow-up<br>• Creates overly difficult learning challenges |

Adapted from CLC (2008).

# External Mentor Pools

Using external mentor pools for a mentoring program often creates unique challenges in recruiting, developing, and managing mentor populations. External mentors bring a different perspective and help learners expand their networks, which make them beneficial for programs that need outside expertise. They can also help provide an objective view of situations within the organization that challenge the learners. In addition, some organizations use an external mentor pool because there aren't enough skilled mentors internally to fulfill the program's need.

The biggest challenge in working with external mentor pools is that they have little motivation to comply with program procedures and processes. Most mentors who are willing to give of their time to develop others have every intention of performing the role well, but sometimes schedules fill up, work gets busy, personal issues arise, and before you know it, that external mentor is prioritizing other things above program requirements, such as surveys and assessments. They'll usually fulfill their obligations, but occasionally someone may struggle with the commitment. Unfortunately, program administrators generally do not have much leverage to get an external mentor who has dropped the ball back on the right path. While this is a risk, keep in mind that the benefits of having external mentors with an outside perspective may outweigh the risks, depending on the context of your program.

The best way to ensure that an external mentor pool stays dedicated to the program is to consider what motivation and resources you can provide to make their effort worthwhile. Unique planning and productivity tools, communication-style assessments, and skills development opportunities are great ways to show mentors they are valued. Mentors generally have more buy-in to the program if they are receiving something substantial in the way of professional growth. Some organizations compensate external mentors for their time. While not always necessary, having a financial component does tangibly demonstrate how important the program is to the organization.

In addition, recognition goes a long way with external mentors. Sending mentors plaques or other symbols of gratitude to display shows your appreciation and allows mentors to show off their accomplishment to others. Or you could send a more personalized gift; for example, if the program is focused on making leaders more effective at leading remote teams, you could send out monogrammed presentation remotes or phone headsets as a fun twist on a traditional gift.

# Communication

Communication is key to setting expectations, increasing awareness about the program for potential mentors, keeping the program and its outcomes front of mind for current mentors, and providing a means of contacting program administrators when issues arise for mentors.

Clear, thorough, and frequent communication is just as much a part of the recipe for success in a mentoring program as any other component. Consider communication content and methods before the launch, during the launch, throughout the program cycle, and at the conclusion of the cycle, if applicable. At each stage, consider what your mentors need to know to perform their role effectively, and what questions they might have that need clarification. Also, think about the obstacles mentors might encounter at each stage, and proactively provide support. For example, during the program cycle, you might expect some learners to start losing momentum and get too busy to keep up with regular mentoring meetings. You can provide email templates for mentors to use to reconnect with these learners.

Plan for checkpoints throughout the program for all stakeholders, including mentors, learners, and their supervisors. Consider what each group needs or wants to know at each stage and then create an appropriate message for each. Table 6-2 is a simple communication plan, which you can customize for your program.

## Resource Materials

Welcome packets and other materials provide a go-to resource for learners and mentors. All materials created for your mentoring program should look professional and be free of any typos or mistakes. Remember, program participants will be using these materials, so they should be clear enough to stand on their own without explanation. They should also be designed in a way that is intuitive and easy to navigate.

### Mentoring Program Welcome Guide

A welcome guide varies in size and complexity, depending on the formality and structure of your program. If the program has many different aspects, assignments, and due dates, the welcome guide will probably need to be more robust than one for a more informal program. Welcome guides can include a welcome message from organizational leadership, the program purpose statement, program design and logistics, list of whom to contact, and key supporting tools and templates. Appendix E has more information about welcome guides.

## Table 6-2. Sample Communication Plan

| Stakeholder (who needs the information?) | Message Content (what do they need or want to know?) | Message Method (what is the best way to share it?) | Timing and Frequency (when and how often?) | Concerns (what questions need to be answered?) |
|---|---|---|---|---|
| Mentor Pool | • Program format<br>• Registration information<br>• Charter information | Webinar (recorded) | 2 months before the launch | • Where to register<br>• Mentor role effort |
| Learner Pool | • Program format<br>• Registration information | Webinar (recorded) | 1 month before the launch | • Where to register<br>• Program logistics |
| Selected Mentors and Learners | • Program launch sequence<br>• Action items | Email with links to resources on intranet | 2 weeks before launch send email<br><br>1 week before and at launch send reminder | • What do I need to do when?<br>• With whom should I meet? |
| Learner Supervisors | • Program structure<br>• Requirements | Email | 2 weeks before the launch | • What is my direct report going to do? |

## First Meeting Guide

A first meeting guide usually provides instructions about setting up and managing the first contact. It is especially helpful in programs with less common structures, such as peer or mentor-led groups, or those with hybrid structures. The first meeting guide provides answers to many frequently asked questions: Who should contact whom? How should the conversation go? What needs to be accomplished? In addition, it should include ideas for developing relationships—such as a list of topics to help establish a personal connection or encouragement to discuss why they were matched—and any assessments or bios used in the matching process.

## Mentor and Learner Job Descriptions

One of the most common questions mentoring program participants have is about their role as mentor or learner. A resource that explains both of these roles to the participants will provide some clarification on expectations for each party (Figure 6-1).

## Figure 6-1. Learner and Mentor Job Responsibilities

| LEARNER | MENTOR |
| --- | --- |
| A learner in XYZ organization has the responsibility to take charge of her own developmental experiences. The learner is expected to have ownership over the direction and content of the mentoring relationship. Learners can expect to spend 10–12 hours per month on their partnership. | A mentor in XYZ organization has the responsibility to sponsor, coach, and facilitate the development of her assigned mentee(s). Mentors are expected to share their expertise, connect mentees with their network, and provide guidance when possible. Mentors can expect to spend 6–10 hours a month on each mentoring relationship. |
| **Responsibilities:**<br><br>• Fully engage in the relationship<br>• Be open to constructive feedback<br>• Set meetings and agendas<br>• Follow up on action items<br>• Identify and track goals<br>• Align key lessons learned with your own situation | **Responsibilities:**<br><br>• Meet on a regular basis<br>• Be available for unscheduled conversations<br>• Give quality feedback<br>• Provide positive facilitation and development experiences |

## Conversation Starters and Questions

Mentoring relationships usually get started without any issue, but there's always a moment when participants have trouble carrying the conversation forward or moving on to a new subject. Help prevent this from happening by providing a list of conversation starters or great questions, such as:

- What is most challenging for this task, skill, or goal?
- What effect could your performance improvement have on your work team?
- Tell me about a time you were in a similar situation. What was the result?
- What transferrable skills or experience do you have?
- Tell me about the obstacles you are facing with this task, skill, or goal.
- What is the consequence of not growing in this skill?
- Who do you know that does this really well?

## Mentor's Playbook

Give your mentors specialized information so they can be as effective as possible. This playbook could contain skill development resources, a thorough explanation of program topics, or lists of learner assignment ideas. You could also include in-depth descriptions of program-related skills and competencies, along with prescribed activities and challenges that can help in their development. This resource will help mentors feel more confident in their ability to be effective.

## Notes and Agenda Templates

Mentors and learners will always appreciate easy-to-use templates. Participants feel more supported when you provide blank versions of note-taking tools and meeting agendas and directions for how to use them. As a bonus, participants may then send you any tools that they create. Eventually, this could result in a crowdsourced set of tools that is perfect for your mentoring program.

# Creating Community

Mentoring programs influence people's lives outside the classroom and often outside the reach of the talent management function. Creating the support resources listed in this chapter is a great way to give participants a good foundation on which to build their mentoring relationships. But there is another very important aspect that can turn a "good" program into a "great" one—community.

Learners and mentors often learn just as much from one another as they do from program administrators and leaders about successful mentoring relationships. Creating a sense of community among the participants is key to accomplishing the purpose of your mentoring program. It also helps increase the value of the program and alleviates administrative requirements. But how do you actually create a community for your learners and mentors?

## Learner Community Events: Reflection Cafe

During the mentoring program, a lot of learning and development occurs in one-on-one or group relationships. Of course, that's the purpose of the program. But there's potential for an even larger gain if they come together outside their formal relationships to collectively and collaboratively examine what they've learned. One way to encourage that community is to host a Reflection Cafe for learners during the program cycle.

Reflection Cafes can come in many forms, but for our purposes they are gatherings of learners who critically review how they've grown through their mentoring relationships. As individuals and then in groups, participants use higher-level critical thinking to draw connections between individual learning and how that can benefit the broader team and organization. A program administrator or leader usually facilitates the Reflection Cafe to keep the group on track.

These events can really be fun if you get creative. For example, if the Reflection Cafe happens at the end of the calendar year, create a cozy atmosphere and have learners decorate gingerbread men to represent some of the key things they learned. Even though these events are social and informal, the conversations will be insightful and the learners will gain a lot. Reflection Cafes not only solidify individual learning and embed it deeper into the organization, but also create an atmosphere of community among the learners. After hosting a few Reflection Cafe events, you'll find that learners stop waiting for a "formal" event and begin having these collaborative conversations on their own.

## Mentor Community Events: Super–Mentor Groups

Many mentors, even senior executives, enjoy receiving validation about what they are doing, learning from one another, trading stories about what's working and what's not, and sharing ideas about how to improve their skills. One way to facilitate this is through super-mentor groups, which are peer-mentoring groups designed to create an open discussion where mentors in the program come together privately and learn from one another. You can often mimic the design and structure of your mentoring program, which has the added benefit of providing similar experiences to your mentors as your learners have in the main program.

Super-mentor groups are best led by either an executive leader, such as the project sponsor, or volunteer mentors from the main program who have outstanding evaluation scores. There are benefits to either choice.

An executive leader can help drive strategic messaging and provide a strategic perspective. This allows you to involve high-influence individuals who may otherwise not have a reason to interact with the program. It also creates more buy-in with influential leaders, and distributes the program's influence to a greater audience because mentors are likely to pass on an executive leader's message to their learners. In addition, mentors typically view this as a beneficial investment in their development because they have access to a high-level mentor.

Alternatively, volunteer leaders have a lot of credibility because they've already proved successful in the mentoring role. This is a great way to publicly recognize these high performers. It also encourages those mentors with highly developed skills to share their processes and experience so that more mentors can achieve greater impact.

Super-mentor groups are a great way to establish community among mentors, share best practices, and raise the level of skill across your mentoring program.

## Leader-Led Community Events: The Team Rally

Sometimes it makes the most sense to create a feeling of community across all participants. For example, in many program designs an individual can participate in several
different mentoring relationships—sometimes as a mentor and sometimes as a learner.
In these types of programs, it can be unnecessarily complicated to break out separate
community events by "mentor" or "learner" labels. A larger group community may
also be appropriate for certain program purposes. For example, if an organization is
trying to improve on innovation, change management, or engagement aspects of the
culture, it will benefit greatly from an inclusive, collaborative support community.

One type of event that helps encourage community across learners and mentors
is a team rally led by executive leadership. These events bring together mentors,
learners, and sometimes their supervisors for collaboration and knowledge sharing. The tone and spirit of these gatherings is often about coming together to open
communication and build more relationships. However, the events can also tackle
specific agenda items. Reflection Cafes and similar activity structures work well at a
team rally. Like other design choices, a team rally event should match the culture of
your organization and have a tone of encouragement and motivation.

# Program Administration

The final aspect of supporting mentoring program participants is the program's
administration. A common pitfall for program designers is to develop a complicated
program that requires massive effort from program administrators, only to find that
no one can take on the extra work.

Program administrators are responsible for the program's day-to-day opera-
tion—from prelaunch communications to post-program cycle reporting. Each design
decision from the Design the Experience step of the AXLES model affects the role
and duties of program administrators.

Depending on the size of your organization, team, and budget, you might have
an individual dedicated to the ongoing maintenance of your formal mentoring
program, or it may simply be one of many responsibilities assigned to someone on
the team. The main requirements to be effective in administering the program are:

- Customer service: Being responsive, respectful, and helpful to all
  participants in the program and stakeholders is key to a positive
  experience.
- Organization: Attention to detail, documentation, being systematic
  in work processes, and hitting deadlines are all important to keeping
  mentoring programs running smoothly.

- Capacity: Having enough bandwidth to devote to the needs of the program is important. Smaller programs (such as informal peer group programs of 20 people) require considerably less time on average than large programs (such as 450 people in a formal one-on-one program). However, every program's needs are unique.

Administrators should be prepared for the ongoing attention that comes with an effective mentoring program. Participants will come in and out of the program, have questions, and encounter issues that need to be resolved. To support the best possible learning experience, administrators need to be highly responsive, diplomatic, and customer service–oriented because they are the face of the program.

Large, complex programs may have a dedicated program administrator, or program manager, who can prioritize his time spent on the program and be responsive to all emerging issues. However, most programs are managed by talent development specialists with an already full workload. In these organizations, those program administrators have the challenging task of juggling the unpredictable needs of mentoring program participants with their other responsibilities. In those situations, keep in mind that the learning experience of someone reaching out for help is very much affected by the customer service she receives.

It is very common to underestimate a mentoring program's administration needs. Overall, the more participants in your program, the more effort required of program administrators. In addition, many aspects of administration take more resources for one-on-one programs (or those that include a hybrid one-on-one structure) than group structures. The following list shows 10 typical program administrator duties and some ideas on estimating the level of effort required.

- Communications: Create a communication plan that includes prelaunch, launch, program cycle, and conclusion communications for all stakeholder groups. Include time to write drafts, edit, and approve.
- Recruiting: The larger the potential pool of learners and mentors, the more time it will take to reach everyone and get applications or registrations. This is also the marketing step, so program administrators may be making calls or attending team meetings to drum up interest in the program.
- Participant Matching: If matching is done manually by program administrators, or collaboratively with participants, assume a large level of initial effort to gather assessments, IDPs, or relevant data and make the first round of matches. Always include time and effort for revising matches based on unexpected issues, such as last-minute requests.

- Mentor Preparation: If program administrators are also mentoring SMEs, they will be doing some of the work to prepare and develop mentors. For each approach to development (communication, webinars, and readings) keep in mind the time needed to not only deliver the solution, but also design and develop it.

- Reporting: A dedicated effort will be required to gather all ongoing regular reporting identified in the evaluation plan, such as learner IDP goals, number of relationships, and goal progress. Much of the Level 1 and Level 2 steps require continuous monitoring and reporting.

- Materials Maintenance: Any materials provided in print or digital form will need regular revision. Those materials that include specific names (project sponsors or program contacts), numbers (program year or contact phone numbers), and organizational knowledge (product names or initiatives) will need to be reviewed closely at least annually. Overall, materials will need to be improved as the program matures and participants provide feedback.

- Emergent Issues: All mentoring programs will have unforeseen obstacles, such as emergency removal of mentors and necessary structure changes. These emerging issues require program administrators who are nimble and responsive, but it also means they should expect to spend an unknown amount of time on those issues. In general, the more participants in the program, the more time required.

- Measuring Effectiveness: In addition to reporting, program administrators will need to interpret data to gain insights, and gather information on Level 3: Performance and Level 4: Results. Data gathering and reporting is ineffective without someone to create the success story. Administrators will need to set gather data, which are often difficult to get, and then analyze any trends and important insights.

- Program Conclusion: Activities related to the end of calendar-based program cycles vary for each unique mentoring program. Consider all concluding activities, such as final evaluations, last meetings, communications, and program-wide events like webinars.

- Program Updates: No mentoring program should remain completely static over time. Insights gained from evaluation are used to find ways to incrementally improve the program design, materials, or support for participants. Time will be spent annually or even quarterly to determine how and when to update the program for maximum effectiveness.

# Support Your Mentors—The Foundation for Results

Jean Williams, Founder, Williams Consulting Group

I was 27 years old and working as a management consultant with my freshly minted business degree from Northwestern's Kellogg Graduate School of Management. This was back in the days when a facsimile machine was *the* modern technological marvel. With a closet of new suits, my leather suitcase, and my consultant title, I thought I was pretty hot stuff.

At some point within that first year, a group of fellow consultants and I completed a team exercise called Desert Survival. For this exercise, each individual read a page of a scenario where we were all in a plane that had crashed in the desert. We had all survived, but we had to prioritize the 10 items that we would keep from the wreckage to help us survive. We each created our "top 10" list individually. Then as a group we discussed our rankings and re-created a group rank list—which is typically a better list than any of the individual lists—with the exercise objective being to exemplify the power of teams.

I grew up camping throughout the United States and was quite experienced with outdoor survival techniques. Therefore, the rank listing was quite easy for me. As the group discussion unfolded, I threw in an opinion or two, but mostly sat back and listened, thinking "there isn't anyone here who has ever spent a night in the woods—let alone the desert. This is rather amusing." When all was said and done, I ended up with a better rank order than the team. I thought I was so smart.

While I had been with this consulting company, I had developed a friendly relationship with a partner, I'll call him P.K., who was about a decade older than me. We would jog together at lunch, and his was the first door I knocked on when I needed advice or wanted to announce a triumph. So after the Desert Survival exercise was finished, I went into P.K.'s office and said, "Hey, I won! I just did better than the team." P.K. looked up from his desk, quietly said, "No, you failed, and you left your team dead in the desert," and then turned back to the report he was reading.

A dozen words. It's hard to believe that they have continued to inform and influence my life ever since. What P.K. pointed out was that being "right" is not worth anything if you don't have the communication skills and influence to bring people along with you. My ability to effectively communicate my thoughts is a skill I have worked on ever since. And there will always be room for improvement.

I was lucky to find P.K. as a mentor when I did. Prior to joining the consulting firm, P.K. had been a professor at the University of Virginia's Darden School of Business, which is where I think he developed his mentoring skills. P.K. knew how to listen without interruption, when to challenge me, and when it was best to let me learn on my own. He wasn't afraid to tell me the truth, even if I didn't want to hear it, because he knew that it would help me. I believe this is one of the most important things about being an effective mentor: The desire to help should always trump the desire to be liked. Had P.K.'s primary intent been to be liked, he would have congratulated me on my superior intelligence. Because he wanted to help me, he was willing to risk having me dislike him by telling the truth. I have had other mentors since P.K., and all have espoused telling the truth that will help.

What is the point of this story? To show that really effective mentors are essential to your development. If you are fortunate enough to have someone in your workplace who is more experienced and wiser than you, listen to what that person says. I didn't like hearing what P.K. said, and I probably left his office in a huff. But he was honest enough to point out a key lead-ership flaw of mine, and it has served me well ever since. Mentors like P.K. give of their time, experience, effort, network, and wisdom for the betterment of others. The best mentors don't do it for recognition, but they should at least be supported. This work is noble, and it is one of the most effective employee development options we have to achieve organizational results. We owe it to our mentors to give them all the tools and resources they need to continue doing this critical work.

# Conclusion

This final step of the AXLES model continues the work needed to support mentors and learners in their experience. Unlike classroom training, the mentoring learning process extends beyond the program, and participants have high expectations for communication, materials, program administration, and community.

Part of offering the support needed for a mentoring program is to develop the skills of your mentor pool. This is an important way to ensure the program will achieve its goals. A positive mentoring experience is dependent on mentors who learn effective skills.

Another important investment in supporting participants of your mentoring program is creating a plan for communication. Think about all the stakeholders who need or want to be informed, and the best way to work with them. Because participants will be referencing materials, such as welcome guides, in isolation from program administrators, you should give special consideration to their design. Make sure they're professional, edited for proper grammar, and reviewed for clarity. Include as much relevant information as possible without overwhelming participants.

Finally, invest in administrative support that can be responsive to the ongoing needs of mentors and learners. Mentoring programs that over-promise support, but are not able to deliver, often fail because participants feel isolated and disengaged. Find the necessary resources to support participants, and re-evaluate this aspect of program customer service often.

Part of the reason mentoring programs are such effective development tools is because learning happens in deep, trusting relationships that extend over time, enabling learners to experiment and work with mentors to adjust their approach. This sustained learning process needs much more support than other types of development to create positive learning experiences and ultimately achieve success for the program.

## Key Insights: Develop Support

1. As an extended learning experience, mentoring programs require more ongoing support to be successful.
2. During this step, you will provide learners and mentors with the resources and materials they need to have a positive learning experience.
3. Invest in developing the skills of your program's mentor pool.
4. Use prelaunch webinars, role play, skills focus, and readings to help increase the effectiveness of mentors.
5. When using external mentor pools, consider providing access to unique and valuable development opportunities to increase buy-in for the program.
6. Frequent, clear communication is mission critical to effective programs. Design a communication plan to include all stakeholders and points of contact.
7. Materials should be designed to include all program-relevant information so participants can access everything they need without contacting a program administrator.
8. Build community among program participants through specially designed events.
9. Program administrators should have an expectation of the amount of ongoing effort required by the program; failing to have administrative support is catastrophic for mentoring programs.
10. Use a well-designed and thorough program welcome guide to give participants all the information they need to grow through mentoring relationships.

# Chapter Exercises

## Mentor Preparation

- What information should you provide to your mentors before program launch that will help them prepare for their role? How will you communicate this information?
- What opportunities will you provide to mentors for practicing their skills?

- Will you use a monthly skills focus, mentor highlights, readings, or assignments to prepare mentors in your program? How will you communicate these resources?
- If mentors in your program are external, what unique considerations should you take into account when preparing to support them?

## Communication

- Who are the stakeholders in your organization who will need communication throughout the life cycle of the mentoring program?
- What information should be distributed to those stakeholders?
- What method of delivery is best for each group of stakeholders?
- When should you communicate with each group? (For example, during design and development, before the program launch, at launch, during the program cycle, at the conclusion of program, or after the program.)
- What is each stakeholder's (or stakeholder group's) concerns or questions?

## Materials

In the table below, list the materials you will need to design and develop for your mentoring program. For each item, identify who will create it, the intended audience, and resources that will contribute to those materials.

| Item | Creator | Audience (mentors, learners, all participants) | Resources (program charter, purpose statement) |
|---|---|---|---|
| | | | |
| | | | |
| | | | |
| | | | |
| | | | |
| | | | |
| | | | |

# 7

# Final Thoughts

What you're doing now, or have done in the past, need not
determine what you can do next and in the future.
—Sir Ken Robinson

## Mentoring Programs Are All About the Experience

This book has illustrated some of the many ways that formal mentoring programs
differ from other types of talent development. The most important differentiator is
that the sustained learning experience is key to achieving results. A positive experience created with skilled mentors, supportive program administration, thoughtful
design, and alignment with the organizational culture is the only way to achieve the
goals you want your mentoring program to attain.

Because mentoring relationships within your program will occur outside a structured physical or virtual classroom, participants will rely on the design and development of your mentoring program to provide all the tools and support they need to
grow their skills and improve performance.

All efforts to communicate effectively, onboard participants into the program
meaningfully, support participants and provide resources, and measure effectiveness
will shape the outcome of the mentoring program. Therefore, the most important
action you can take when creating your mentoring program is to invest tremendous
effort in building a positive experience for all participants within your program—
both learners and mentors.

## The AXLES Model for Developing Mentoring Programs

Because mentoring programs are, by definition, sustained learning processes rather
than one-off events, you need to take a more effective approach to designing them.

The AXLES model guides practitioners along the thought process for developing aligned, sustainable, and scalable mentoring programs.

Throughout chapters 2 through 6 of this book, you examined each of components closely:

- Align to a Purpose
- Design the Experience
- Launch the Program
- Evaluate Effectiveness
- Support Participants.

Because the model isn't linear, work can be ongoing in several of the steps at once. In fact, none of the steps is ever truly finished—you should expect to continue adjusting and updating the program throughout its lifetime to keep it aligned and current within the organization.

## Align to a Purpose

The Align to a Purpose phase is that critical foundational piece that everyone wants to skip. However, it's imperative that you don't because this is when you position yourself as a critical partner to best define success for the program. You also set the stage for success by making sure you (as a project lead) and your teams have access to the project sponsor and other senior leaders so you can get invaluable insight and elicit support for the program. Use your conversations with senior leaders to make sure you are identifying and targeting the organization's most critical talent needs. This ensures that the program is providing the highest value possible.

In highly hierarchical organizations, practitioners may feel helpless if they don't have direct access to stakeholders and leadership. This can be addressed by acting as a consultative partner and explaining the potential negative impact of the situation. If senior leaders seem to be worried that you'll waste their time, you can promise to take up less than 10 minutes per week. (And then make sure you deliver!) If your boss doesn't like you going over her head, ask her to sit in with you in the meetings to contribute to the project. Sometimes, gaining access is as simple as asking for it.

Another aspect of this phase is defining mentoring for the organization. Is your organization's program defined or more individualized? Is there a strong distinction between coaching and mentoring? The definition of mentoring will often (but not always) clarify important design factors, such as structure and whether programs are voluntary or optional.

Finally, this phase of the AXLES model comes together in the purpose statement deliverable, which is a tool that helps define the mentoring program and the factors to consider for measuring the success of the mentoring program.

# Design the Experience

The second phase of the AXLES model starts us on the path of design. This phase or step can and should be done in conjunction with other parts of the model, rather than as a linear process. Mentoring relationships do not work in a straight line, so you shouldn't expect the model to do so either. Approach the mentoring program's design with some flexibility. While many decisions can be determined in order, you'll find that iterative adjustments should be made occasionally. This creates a fluid process that results in high-impact mentoring programs.

In the Design the Experience step, we look at five major design decisions:

- Structure: This is the bones of the program. Will one-on-one relationships work best for your program's purpose, or is reverse mentoring better? Maybe a mentor-led group or peer mentoring would be the best approach for accomplishing the goals of the program. Ultimately, many practitioners find that a combination or hybrid structure best addresses learner and mentor needs.

- Schedule: There is a wide variety of choices for scheduling the program, but most fall into open (inclusive, never-ending), calendar-based (in which the program starts and ends at specific times throughout the year), or programmatic (tied to other organizational events).

- Matching: Learners and mentors can be matched based on a spectrum of possible approaches. Should learners self-select mentors, or is it better for administrators to match participants based on role and location data? Or would an entirely different approach work better? The best choice for your program depends on your organizational culture and the program's goals.

- Learner Participation: The three Es of participation are entry, exit, and expectations. How do learners get involved with the program? In what (planned and unplanned) way might they leave the program? What is expected of them during their time within the program?

- Mentor Participation: As with learner participation, mentor participation also focuses on the three Es. How are you planning to bring mentors into the program, how will they leave, and what will they be expected to do as part of their role?

After all the design work is completed, you will bring it together in the program charter, which is the documented vision of what the program looks like and how it will run. The charter is an agreement between the project team members and project sponsors and stakeholders about the direction the program's development will take.

## Launch the Program

Unlike training events, a mentoring program launch is not the end result of your design and development work; it's simply the moment that participants become involved. Because mentoring programs are sustained learning processes that need to be supported over the long term, the program launch is a small but critical piece to ensure program success. Program launch events help learners and mentors prepare for their relationships, get excited, and engage with a different type of learning experience. It is an important marker, where participants expect to learn critical program information and find out about resources that will set them up for success.

The format of the launch event is entirely dependent on the program's purpose and what is best for the experience of your participants. Depending on your organizational culture and the program's structure and schedule, the launch might be an epic, live event, with all participants sent off-site for an all-day mentoring workshop; it could also be a more relaxed, asynchronous virtual onboarding experience; or anything in between.

The launch event is also the best time to begin earning a reputation for frequent, clear, and consistent communication with your learners, mentors, and stakeholders. By the time you have designed the program launch, you should have an agenda that describes the format of the launch, and a specific plan for all prelaunch communications.

## Evaluate Effectiveness

Even though much of the talent development industry continues to consider evaluation an afterthought, the AXLES model strives to define success and effectiveness from the very beginning. During the first phase of the model, Align to a Purpose, the program's success was defined and included in the program purpose statement. As you continue to work through the design and development of the program, that definition of success should serve as your singular goal.

Long before you put the program into place, you want to have a plan for how to measure effectiveness within the program. The New World Kirkpatrick Model works well for measuring mentoring programs. You can use:

- Level 1: Reaction to look at learner satisfaction, engagement, and relevance
- Level 2: Learning to identify how well learners grew as a result of their mentoring relationship(s)
- Level 3: Behavior as a measurement of performance growth on the job
- Level 4: Results to help show you whether the program hit its intended goals as defined at the beginning of the design work.

The most important thing to remember about the effectiveness step is that, like every other aspect of the mentoring program process, this is not a one-and-done approach. Instead, plan frequent and consistent status checks to get leading indicators of the program's effectiveness. This approach allows you to make minor but valuable course corrections to improve the program's overall results.

Finally, use a varied approach to gather multiple sources of data over time to illustrate the program's story of success. One point-in-time piece of data doesn't have enough depth to create a narrative of how the participants are doing in their sustained learning process. Therefore, you make evaluating effectiveness a sustained process, allowing you to gain valuable insight into the program's success.

## Support Participants

The final step in developing effective mentoring programs is to provide support for all participants in the program. From the time they get started in the program until the time they leave, learners and mentors will require information, resources, and help to co-create a positive developmental experience. The possibilities are endless; some common resources include videos, articles, books, online modules, and job aids. Learners and mentors will appreciate any materials that help them to navigate their roles successfully.

In addition, you should place a special emphasis on developing the skills of your mentor pool. Mentors are the linchpin of your mentoring program, so it is a wise investment to put effort into their skills development. If you have an external mentor pool, they will take even more energy to support throughout the mentoring program cycle. External mentors can sometimes require a bit more wrangling than an internal group, so make sure to allocate bandwidth for that effort.

When talking about support, not enough can be said about the importance of communicating with learners, mentors, and other stakeholders. Everyone is going to want to know what to expect and when, and most people will have concerns or questions they need answered. Plan ahead for specific communication checkpoints to avoid losing touch.

Most of all, it is critical to be proactive about estimating program administration needs and allocating resources accordingly. A mistake common among failed programs is to launch without the required administrative resources available. For example, large, complex, formal mentoring programs often require at least one full-time administrator to fully support participants. Without that available support, the program won't be able to sustain a positive experience and support will decrease. A positive learning experience includes access to responsive program support—

participants can come up with some very interesting dilemmas, issues, and questions, and you want to make sure someone is available to help get through it.

## Old Is New Again

There are many reasons why mentoring programs are ineffective. Some were held over from previous leadership teams or initiatives. Others were originally created to address talent needs that changed over time, but no one repurposed and updated the program to focus on current talent issues.

Ineffective programs and programs that have lost momentum will affect your ability to develop talent. These programs tarnish the organization's reputation for credible mentoring, and make you (as a practitioner) seem out of touch. They should either be fixed or discarded.

Use the AXLES model to diagnose the issues with broken programs. Are they out of alignment? Fostering mediocre or poor experiences? Is there a lack of support? (Or likely all of the above?) Once you've figured out the issues, use the AXLES model to make these programs effective again.

## Break the Cycle of Failure

Dated and ineffective programs are not the only problem—most programs being developed today are still missing critical pieces to ensure success. Sometimes they are incomplete experiences or not aligned to address the most critical talent needs of the organization. Very often, there is little or no support for mentors and learners to perform their roles. Mentoring programs may seem like an easy solution to address complex talent issues, but in reality, they require a tremendous amount of effort to implement successfully.

What you get out of your mentoring program is proportional to what you put into it. Programs that don't align to the organization's top needs, are not designed for scalability and sustainability, or lack involvement from top stakeholders and sponsors are ultimately doomed to fail.

## Forward With Purpose and Awareness

At the end of the day, mentoring programs are so popular because they can get results. The connections people make within these programs are challenging, sustaining, inspiring, and life changing; ultimately, they increase the capability and performance of the workforce.

For these reasons, it's a good idea to continue delivering formal mentoring programs within your organization to help address your most critical talent needs.

But remember, while mentoring programs can certainly address many fundamental talent issues, they ultimately fail because you don't address common obstacles and mistakes, such as lack of:

- alignment to the organization's top talent needs
- planning for program scalability and sustainability
- sponsor or stakeholder involvement and support.

Using the AXLES Model will help you avoid these mistakes because it ensures alignment to top talent needs, designs for an experience that is scalable and sustainable, and uses deliverables such as the program charter to involve stakeholders throughout the process. Successful mentoring programs are those that have been developed to align with a specific organizational purpose, designed to create the best possible learning experience, launched to effectively onboard participants, frequently evaluated for effectiveness, and tirelessly provided support to learners and mentors.

A tremendously effective mentoring program is not going to be easy to design, develop, and execute. However, the results are worth it. As you continue your journey to develop and deliver a great mentoring program, continuously search for ways to improve the participant experience and support the sustained learning process. The programs that always seek iterative improvements to stay aligned with the organization and participant needs are the ones that succeed and last.

## You Need a Mentor Too!

Finally, as you prepare to move forward with the tools and resources in this book, consider how you (and your team) will find ways to grow. If you want to craft and support the best possible mentoring experiences for your participants, you should also seek and work with a mentor.

Throughout my career, I have sought and worked with a lot of mentors, and I am never surprised by how much I gain from those discussions. The experience of having a mentoring relationship (or several) can provide the personal insights that you need to bring back to your program to improve it further.

Those in charge of developing talent tend to be the last to participate in development activities themselves, so I encourage you to jump in and demonstrate exactly what effective mentoring relationships can look like.

# Alignment Tools

## Alignment and Discovery Meeting Agenda

The goal of an alignment and discovery meeting is to determine the purpose of your mentoring program and how you will achieve its goals. Your meeting should focus on the following:

1. What is the ideal state we are trying to achieve with the mentoring program?
   - In what observable ways will performance be improved? (Specify performance factors.)
   - How will employees feel or think differently?
2. What is the current state of the specified performance factors? (Think about attrition, shallow talent bench strength, learning curve, and long time to success in critical jobs.)
   - Why?
   - What is the current state of mentoring within the organization?
3. What constraints will the program face?
   - What resources are available?
   - What's the impact of the culture on program design decisions?
   - What are the time constraints for designing and implementing the program?
   - What are the time constraints of participants once the program is launched?
4. Make the case for a mentoring program at the organization.
   - How can we change the business need into a positive?
   - Make this the strategic goal of the mentoring program.
5. What does success look like?
   - How will we measure progress?

- What indicators of success will be available throughout the program?
- What incremental changes do we want to see?

## Alignment and Discovery Meetings

The following questions include additional clarification, but are otherwise identical to those listed in chapter 2.

1. What did not work well about this program? What worked well and is important to keep in the next iteration? (For programs needing redesign)

2. Be sure to consider aspects of the program development process and the participant experience. What specific feedback did you receive about participant recruitment and onboarding? Matches? Meetings? How was effectiveness measured previously?

3. What attributes of the organization's culture should be captured for the program? (Consider mission, vision, and values and other documents.)

4. Typically, it is advised to review strategic documents such as the organization's mission and vision statements and core values. Other relevant documents might include department or operating group strategy, annual goals, and company-wide initiatives from the previous two years.

5. How should mentoring be defined for this organization? (Use descriptive phrases wherever possible.)

6. Encourage stakeholders to use observable terms. Does mentoring occur "between a more experienced employee and a less experienced one" or does it occur "in organic working relationships." Observable behavior makes it easier to measure effectiveness later!

7. What are the organization's most critical talent needs? (Limit to one primary and up to three secondary needs.)

8. Here are some common examples, but use language that resonates with your stakeholders:
   - high attrition
   - low engagement
   - sharp learning curve
   - long time to success in role
   - diluted or undefined culture
   - shallow talent bench
   - difficulty recruiting top talent
   - low diversity and inclusion
   - lack of strategic thinking.

9.  How can we make the business case for a mentoring program? What are the solutions (part or whole) that this mentoring program will bring to the organization?

10. Change the critical talent needs listed above into a positive. Our examples become:

    - increased retention
    - increased engagement
    - smooth learning curve
    - decreased time to success in role
    - clear, strong culture
    - deep and broad talent bench
    - improved recruiting of top talent
    - measurable diversity and inclusion
    - competency in strategic thinking.

11. What benefits are possible for mentors and learners who participate in the program?

12. What do you want learners to do differently or better as a result of their time in the program? How do you want them to feel or think differently? What do you intend for mentors to be able to do differently or better? How do you want mentors to think or feel differently?

13. What are the quantitative or qualitative measures of success for the mentoring program? (It is OK to draft measures at this point and come back to refine them in later steps.)

14. This last question is to start clarifying success measures, not necessarily to finalize them. It is better to start the conversation at the beginning and refine as you go.

# Mentoring Program Purpose Statement

The tangible deliverable from the Align to a Purpose step is a mentoring program purpose statement. This serves as the first point of agreement among the project sponsor, stakeholders, and project team members.

The benefit of this deliverable is that it is reusable and becomes a go-to resource throughout the project's life cycle. The purpose statement should be included during communications and in materials provided to participants, which are covered in detail in chapter 6. It should also be used in executive status update meetings and as the elevator speech when speaking to stakeholders. It essentially becomes an all-in-one default for how you describe the mentoring program.

Using the responses to the questions you answered in the alignment and discovery meetings, craft a draft program purpose statement. The goal is to create a working document that the project team can agree on, and that will continue to evolve as needed during program development.

Remember your purpose statement might be a few sentences or a few paragraphs and should include the:

- definition of mentoring for the organization
- cultural impact
- talent needs
- business case
- benefits to mentors and learners
- definition of program success.

# The Program Charter

Building off the purpose statement you created in the Align to a Purpose step, the program charter identifies the choices made in the designing the experience phase. A blank template is provided below and an example charter follows.

## Program Charter

| Charter Items | Your Design |
|---|---|
| Purpose Statement<br>*(chapter 2)* | |
| Program Objectives and Benefits<br>*(chapter 2)* | |
| Stakeholders<br>*(chapter 2)* | |
| Mentor Candidates<br>*(chapter 2)* | |
| Learner Candidates<br>*(chapter 2)* | |
| Program Structure<br>*(design decision 1; chapter 3)* | |
| Program Schedule<br>*(design decision 2; chapter 3)* | |
| Participant Matching<br>*(design decision 3; chapter 3)* | |
| Learner Participation<br>*(design decision 4; chapter 3)* | **Entry:**<br>**Expectations:**<br>**Exit:** |
| Mentor Participation<br>*(design decision 5; chapter 3)* | **Entry:**<br>**Expectations:**<br>**Exit:** |
| Expected Investment<br>*(direct costs and hours of investment)* | **Direct costs:**<br>**Hours of investment:** |
| Program Administration<br>*(plan for administrating program design; more in chapter 6)* | |

# Sample Program Charter

| Charter Items | Your Design |
|---|---|
| Purpose Statement | The mentorship program at AcmeTech is designed to encourage branch managers to learn from one another and maintain a strong network, which is central to our culture of learning.<br><br>At AcmeTech, we believe in the impact of individual mentees learning from mentors in a one-on-one relationship built on trust and respect. The mentorship program provides job skill development and opportunities for professional growth to branch managers. Senior leaders who participate as mentors in the program will gain new perspective and insights as a result of their mentoring relationship, and will increase their legacy footprint in the organization.<br><br>This program will help preserve the company culture we have worked hard to build and maintain our high standard for job performance. It will also prepare our branch managers for critical leadership positions during this time of growth. The goal is to ensure a sufficient pool of candidates who are ready to be successful in future leadership positions. |
| Program Objectives and Benefits | • Build talent bench strength<br>• Decrease time to success in critical positions<br>• Increase manager networks<br>• Increase job skill development |
| Stakeholders | • Branch managers<br>• Supervisors<br>• Senior leaders (mentors) |
| Mentor Candidates | Senior leaders (director and above) |
| Learner Candidates | Branch managers |
| Program Structure | One-on-one traditional |
| Program Schedule | Annual (March through August) |
| Participant Matching | Role and location |
| Learner Participation | **Entry:** Interested learners will complete an application in February.<br><br>**Expectations:** Adhere to performance standards, good faith effort toward program and individual goals, and demonstrate respect and ownership in the learning relationship<br><br>**Exit:** Program will conclude in August. Learners may be removed due to poor performance or self-elect to leave program. |
| Mentor Participation | **Entry:** Interested mentors will complete an application in February.<br><br>**Expectations:** Adhere to performance standards, demonstrate investment and effort, and be available for meetings and calls<br><br>**Exit:** Program will conclude in August. Mentors may be removed due to poor evaluations or self-elect to leave program. |

| | |
|---|---|
| Expected Investment | **Direct Costs:**<br>• Instructional Design Vendor: $--<br>• Software Mentor Platform: $--<br>• Launch Event: $--<br><br>**Hours of Investment:**<br>• Mentors can expect to spend between 1 and 2 hours per week on each mentoring relationship for the duration of the program.<br>• Learners can expect to spend between 1 and 4 hours per week for the duration of the program. |

# Launch Event Agendas

The following templates help guide the design of your mentoring program launch event. There is a blank template for a live face-to-face event, and one that works well for virtual or asynchronous program onboarding. A complete sample face-to-face program launch agenda rounds out this appendix.

# Face-to-Face Program Launch

This face-to-face launch agenda template is set up for a one-day event.

| Launch Item | Your Program Detail | Details |
|---|---|---|
| Considerations | Participant Needs:<br><br>Program Structure and Schedule:<br><br>Delivery Constraints: | Participant needs, program structure and schedule, and delivery constraints |
| Prelaunch Communication | | Information and resources needed before program begins |
| Registration | | Plan for registering participants (if applicable) |
| Matching | | Plan for matching mentor relationships before or during the launch |
| Program Launch Design | 8–9 a.m. | Content (program information, goal setting) and activities (paired review, group exercise) |
| | 9–10 a.m. | Content and activity |
| | 10–10:15 a.m. | BREAK |
| | 10:15–11 a.m. | Content and activity |
| | 11 a.m.–12 p.m. | Content and activity |
| | 12–1 p.m. | Social networking lunch |
| | 1–2 p.m. | Content and activity |
| | 2–2:45 p.m. | Content and activity |
| | 2:45–3 p.m. | BREAK |
| | 3–4 p.m. | Content and activity |
| | 4–5 p.m. | Next steps and wrap up |
| Post-Launch Communication | | Information, resources, milestones, due dates, and reinforcement from program launch. |

# Virtual Extended Program Launch

This template is set up for a virtual launch delivery over several smaller sessions. In this template as well as the previous one, the Launch Item column can be adjusted to suit the length and structure of your program.

| Launch Item | Your Program Detail | Description |
|---|---|---|
| Considerations | Participant Needs:<br><br>Program Structure and Schedule:<br><br>Delivery Constraints: | Participant needs, program structure and schedule, and delivery constraints |
| Prelaunch Communication | | Information and resources needed before program begins |
| Registration | | Plan for registering participants (if applicable) |
| Matching | | Plan for matching mentor relationships before or during the launch |
| | | |
| Week 1 | | Introduction to program, content focus, partner or group activity, Q&A (or panel discussion), and next steps |
| Week 2 | | Welcome back, content focus, partner or group activity, and next steps |
| Week 3 | | Welcome back, content focus, partner or group activity, and next steps |
| Week 4 | | Welcome back, content focus, partner or group activity, next steps |
| | | |
| Post-Launch Communication | | Information, resources, milestones, due dates, and reinforcement from program launch webinars |

# Sample Face-to-Face Program Launch Agenda

| Launch Item | Details |
|---|---|
| Considerations | Participant Needs: Geographically dispersed group traveling for launch event. Under pressure because of time out of office.<br><br>Program Structure and Schedule: One-on-one traditional structure, running each March through August.<br><br>Delivery Constraints: Held at an off-site conference location to minimize distractions. |
| Prelaunch Communication | • Provide digital copy of the welcome guide, a letter from the company president, and a calendar of events.<br>• Invite all participants to take an online behavioral assessment (reports to be distributed at launch).<br>• Provided matched mentor and mentee names, as well as a short bio. |
| Registration | Amy S. (Training Coordinator) is managing registration through an online portal. |
| Matching | Chris M. and Martin K. will complete initial matching with the Role and Location method two weeks prior to launch. Matches will be sent by email one week prior to launch. Chris M. will manage any requests or urgent needs as they arise. |
| | |
| 8–9 a.m. | Welcome by the company president (personal story of mentoring success)<br>Icebreaker networking activity |
| 9–10 a.m. | Behavioral assessment debrief and group exercise |
| 10–10:15 a.m. | BREAK |
| 10:15–11 a.m. | First mentor meeting (structured introductions) |
| 11 a.m.–12 p.m. | Mentor paired discussions (World Cafe) |
| 12–1 p.m. | Social networking lunch |
| 1–2 p.m. | Mentoring panel:<br>• Marie B., SVP Sales<br>• Garrett L., Manager Toronto Branch<br>• Alexis R., Manager Pittsburgh Branch<br>Sara S., Associate Payroll |
| 2–2:45 p.m. | Mentor meeting (goal setting and expectations) |
| 2:45–3 p.m. | BREAK |
| 3–4 p.m. | Road mapping group activity |
| 4–5 p.m. | Next steps and wrap-up |
| | |
| Post-Launch Communication: | • Thank-you note from the president<br>• Stats and quotes from the launch meeting<br>• Additional readings<br>• Upcoming milestones and reminders of action items |

# The Evaluation Plan

To best capture a story of success for your program, plan backward through the four levels of evaluation, starting at Level 4 and moving down through Level 1. The template below is a starting point for you to plan your approach. Use the questions provided to flesh out your evaluation plan. Following that are two completed versions you can use as examples.

## Evaluation Plan Template

| | | | | |
|---|---|---|---|---|
| **Level 4: Results** | What strategic results was the program was created to measure? | What qualitative and quantitative metrics can be used to measure results? | When will this be measured? How often? By whom? | Who will review and analyze the data? |
| **Level 3: Behavior** | What learner performance factors or behaviors will ultimately lead to Level 4 success? | What qualitative and quantitative metrics can be used to measure performance? | When will this be measured? How often? By whom? | Who will review and analyze the data? |
| **Level 2: Learning** | What learning leads to demonstrating the Level 3 behaviors needed for success? | What qualitative and quantitative metrics can be used to measure development in knowledge, skills, and attitude? | When will this be measured? How often? By whom? | Who will review and analyze data? |
| **Level 1: Reaction** | What factors of satisfaction and learner engagement will contribute to successful learning in Level 2? | What qualitative and quantitative metrics can be used to measure satisfaction, engagement, and relevance? | When will this be measured? How often? By whom? | Who will review and analyze data? |

# Sample 1 Evaluation Plan

| | | | | |
|---|---|---|---|---|
| **Level 4: Results** | Build a sufficient talent pipeline to address known upcoming leadership openings. | Number of internal promotions versus external hires<br><br>Number of promotions from high-potential group<br><br>Time to success/hit goals | Every three months starting two quarters after program launch by program administrator.<br><br>Metrics captured by HR department. | Program administrator will send out evaluation analysis quarterly, one week after the promotion and hire report is available. |
| **Level 3: Behavior** | Perform defined leadership competencies at a high level of effectiveness on the job. | Manager observations<br><br><br>360-degree feedback results<br><br><br>Performance review results | Observations will be done every two months starting from the third month of the program and continuing 6 months past program.<br><br>360-degree feedback is completed at the start of program, once midprogram, and once at the end.<br><br>Performance reviews conducted annually and gathered from HR and L&D. | Program administrator and program coordinator will divide efforts to analyze observations and 360-degree feedback results, and report on results quarterly.<br><br>Performance review results tracked annually by HR and reported by them. |
| **Level 2: Learning** | Perform defined leadership competencies during course of mentoring relationship. | Mentor observations<br><br><br>360-degree feedback results<br><br><br>Self-assessment | Observations done every 2 months during program.<br><br>360-degree feedback (see above).<br><br>Self-assessments given twice during program. | See above for observations and 360-degree feedback.<br><br>Self-assessments will be recorded and analyzed by the program coordinator. |
| **Level 1: Reaction** | Perceived relevance of mentoring to likelihood of promotion.<br><br>Expected obstacles to career goals.<br><br>Satisfaction with participation in program. | Monthly pulse evaluations, alternating monthly between surveys to 25 percent of participants and focus groups of 25 percent of participants | Surveys to be sent through LMS by program coordinator.<br><br>Focus groups facilitated by project sponsor. | Program coordinator during last week of each month. |

# Sample 2 Evaluation Plan

| | | | | |
|---|---|---|---|---|
| **Level 4: Results** | Build talent bench<br><br>Decrease time to success in critical positions | Executive confidence in the talent pool<br><br>Number of internal versus external hires<br><br>Elapsed time before hitting set target goals<br><br>Known indirect costs of poor leadership transition | Quarterly executive business reviews<br><br>Performance reporting data<br><br>Engagement pulse surveys | Training coordinator Emily will compile data<br><br>CHRO will share reports at quarterly meetings |
| **Level 3: Behavior** | Define leadership competencies according to AcmeTech model. | Supervisor observations<br><br>Multirater assessments<br><br>Performance review results | Quarterly through LMS, conducted by the training coordinator | A dedicated training coordinator |
| **Level 2: Learning** | Perform defined leadership competencies during course of mentoring relationship. | Mentor observations<br><br>Self-assessments<br><br>Previous annual reviews | Observations and self-assessments every two months | Dedicated training coordinator |
| **Level 1: Reaction** | Career goals<br><br>Supervisor support<br><br>Well-defined development goals | Preprogram assessments<br><br>Monthly focus groups and pulse surveys | Surveys to be sent through LMS by program coordinator.<br><br>Focus groups facilitated by project sponsor. | Dedicated training coordinator |

# The Program Welcome Guide

A mentoring program welcome guide is a digital or printed onboarding document with all the tools and resources your participants need to get started in their mentoring relationships. The guide will usually include some standard components (listed below) and a selection of pieces that are specific to the program and your organization.

Use the descriptions below to help determine how best to welcome your participants into your program. Then read through the example welcome guide to see how it all fits together.

## Standard Items:

- welcome letter from executive sponsor
- program purpose statement (or vision and mission statements)
- mentoring philosophy
- mentoring program description (structure and schedule)
- description of learners and mentors
- explanation of matching process
- milestones and due dates
- mentor and learner role expectations
- program administrator contact information.

## Optional Items:

- Individual development plan (IDP) template and instructions
- mentoring agreement template
- mentor and learner job descriptions
- conversation starters
- agenda template
- list of program-specific resources (registration forms)

- list of development resources (articles on mentoring skills)
- competency and skills content.

## Context-Specific Items

- Leadership Development Programs
  - Resources describing leadership behaviors
  - List of additional development
  - Suggested stretch assignments
- New Hire Programs
  - Organizational mission, vision, values
  - Human resources contact information
  - Organization's history and culture
  - Organizational chart
  - Logistical information (where to find new employee handbook)
- Sales/Customer Service Programs
  - Value proposition
  - Product/services descriptions
  - Sales process
  - Best practices for customer discovery

One of the challenges in creating a Program Welcome Guide is striking a balance between providing enough information that participants need and want without giving them a huge manual they will never use. Keep the design of the document simple so that it can easily be updated with new and changing information.

# Welcome Guide Outline

## Welcome Letter From Executive Sponsor
(Includes personal story and why the program is important to organizational strategy.)

## Program Purpose Statement
The mentorship program at AcmeTech is designed to encourage branch managers to learn from each other and maintain a strong network, which is central to our culture of learning. At AcmeTech, we believe in the impact of individual mentees learning from mentors in a one-on-one relationship built on trust and respect. The mentorship program provides job skill development and opportunities for professional growth to branch managers. Senior leaders who participate as mentors in the program will gain new perspective and insights as a result of their mentoring

relationship, and will increase their legacy footprint in the organization. This program will help preserve the company culture we have worked hard to build and maintain our high standard for job performance while preparing our branch managers for critical leadership positions during this time of growth. The goal of this program is to ensure a sufficient pool of candidates who are ready to be successful in future leadership positions.

## Mentoring Program Description

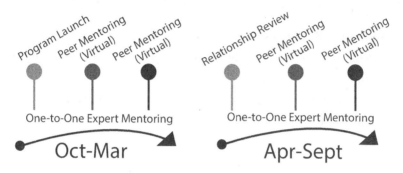

## Our Participants
- Senior leaders (director and above)
- Branch managers

## Matching Process
- All participants will complete an application of interest no later than February 15.
- The talent development team will match mentees with mentors based on stated goals for the relationship and potential mentors' areas of expertise.
- Additional consideration given to location.

## Milestones and Due Dates
- February 15: Applications due
- March 10: Program launch event
- April 1: Initial mentoring agreements due
- April 24: Focus groups and pulse surveys
- May 28: Focus groups and pulse surveys
- June 1: Self-assessments and observations
- July 15: Focus groups and pulse surveys
- August 1: Self-assessments and observations
- August 29: Conclude relationships and final assessments

## Mentor and Learner Role Expectations

- For Learners:
  - Adhere to performance standards
  - Good faith effort toward program and individual goals
  - Demonstrate respect and ownership in the learning relationship
- For Mentors:
  - Adhere to performance standards
  - Demonstrate investment and effort to be available for meetings and calls
- Additional Resources
  - Videos, articles, and other resources available through the learning management system.
  - List of AcmeTech leadership competencies and prescriptives available on the intranet.

## Program Administrator Contact

Amy S., Training Coordinator

619.555.5555

Amys@acmetech.com

# Individual Development Plan Template

An individual development plan (IDP) is a tool to assist career and personal development. It is designed to help employees reach short- and long-term career goals, as well as improve current job performance (OPM n.d.). Use this template as a guide.

| | |
|---|---|
| Date/Version | This is an ongoing process that should be updated regularly. Dating or versioning the document is a good way to track recent changes. |
| Name | |
| Title/Department | Current title or role |
| Desired Next Role | What is the role you would like to reach for next? This may not be a formal title change; it might include additional responsibilities or stretch assignments. |
| Mentor | |
| 3 Strengths | Before thinking about areas for improvement, concentrate on the value you bring to your team and organization. How do you leverage your strengths at work?<br><br>1.<br><br>2.<br><br>3. |
| Development Goal* | Describe your development goal in terms of observable behavior and skills. Explain why you have chosen this goal. Describe how improvement in this goal will help you to perform better and how it will affect your team. |
| Action Items | Use specific and measurable language to identify 1–3 actions you will take to increase progress in your goal. Action items should have listed milestones or due dates. |
| Resources | People, technology, systems, or other items needed to achieve goal. |
| Outcomes | Describe the impact of achieving this goal for yourself and team. |

*Up to three development goals may be included.*

# 9-Box Example

The following example is a fictional 9-box matrix. These data can be used to help match skills for mentoring programs. Individuals listed with a "#" to the left of their name are mentees in the program. In parentheses after the mentees' names is their top developmental goal. Those with a "^" next to their name are mentors. In parentheses after the mentors are their top strengths.

Keep in mind, this fictional example shows a total pool of five mentees and five mentors who are perfectly matched. Typically, this method yields a few people who don't seem to have an easy match, and you may need to recruit additional mentors with specific expertise.

| | Needs Coaching | High Potential. | Future Leader |
|---|---|---|---|
| **High** | # Jason F. (Bus. Acumen)<br># Diana C. (Presenting)<br># Lynn W. (Exec. Presence) | ^ Brigitte G. (Presenting)<br># Greg F. (Accountability) | ^ Marisol E. (Exec. Presence)<br>^ Jorge S. (Accountability) |
| | **Poor Job Fit** | **Well-Placed**<br>^ Garvin S. (Product Sales) | **High Performer**<br>^ John B. (Bus. Acumen) |
| **Potential** | | | |
| **Low** | **Low Performer** | **Contributor**<br>^ Shana W. (Product Sales) | **Needs Development** |
| | Low | Performance | High |

# References

ATD (Association for Talent Development). 2015. "Mentoring and Coaching: Which is Which, and Where Do I Start?" *TD at Work* Job Aid Collection. Alexandria, VA: ATD Press.

CLC (Corporate Leadership Council). 2002. "Mentoring Programs for a Dispersed Work Force." Washington, DC: CLC.

———. 2005. "Mentoring: From Theory to Action." Corporate Leadership Council. March. www.corporateleadershipcouncil.com.

———. 2008. "Mentor and Coach Matching: Understanding Theories and Implementation Tactics for Higher Return." Corporate Leadership Council. March. www.corporateleadershipcouncil.com.

Duarte, N. 2010. *Resonate: Present Visual Stories That Transform Audiences*. Hoboken, NJ: John Wiley & Sons.

Emelo, R. 2015. *Modern Mentoring*. Alexandria, VA: ATD Press.

Harvey, F.J., P.J. Schoomaker, and K.O. Preston. 2005. "Leaving a Legacy Through Mentorship." Memorandum in the *Army Mentorship Handbook*. January 1.

IFC (International Coaching Federation). n.d. "Coaching FAQs." www.coachfederation.org/need/landing.cfm?ItemNumber=978&navItemNumber=567.

Kaye, B., and D. Scheef. 2000. "Mentoring." *Infoline*. Alexandria, VA: ASTD Press.

OPM (U.S. Office of Personnel Management). 2008. *Best Practices: Mentoring*. Washington, DC: OPM. www.opm.gov/policy-data-oversight/training-and-development/career-development/bestpractices-mentoring.pdf.

———. n.d. "Individual Development Plan." OPM's Training and Development Policy Wiki. www.opm.gov/WIKI/training/Individual-Development-Plans.ash.

Phillips-Jones, L. 2003a. *The Mentee's Guide: How to Have a Successful Relationship With a Mentor*. Grass Valley, CA: Mentoring Group.

———. 2003b. *The Mentor's Guide: How to Be the Kind of Mentor You Once Had—Or Wish You'd Had*. Grass Valley, CA: Coalition of Counseling Centers/The Mentoring Group.

———. 2003c. *The Mentoring Coordinator's Guide: How to Plan and Conduct a Successful Mentoring Initiative*. Grass Valley, CA: Mentoring Group.

PMI (Project Management Institute). 2014. *Executive Sponsor Engagement—Top Driver of Project and Program Success*. Pulse of the Profession In-Depth Report. Newtown Square, PA: PMI. www.pmi.org/-/media/pmi/documents/public/pdf/learning/thought -leadership/pulse/executive-sponsor-engagement.pdf.

Reitman, A., and S.R. Benatti. 2014a. *Creating a Mentoring Program: Mentoring Partnerships Across the Generations*. Alexandria, VA: ASTD Press.

———. 2014b. "Mentoring Versus Coaching: What's the Difference?" ATD Human Capital blog, August 8. www.td.org/Publications/Blogs/Human-Capital-Blog/2014/08/ Mentoring-Versus-Coaching-Whats-the-Difference.

U.S. Army. 2006. *Army Leadership: Competent, Confident, and Agile*. FM 6-22. http://usacac.army.mil/cac2/Repository/Materials/fm6-22.pdf.

Way, C., and B. Kaye. 2011. "Tools for Effective Mentoring Programs." *Infoline*. Alexandria, VA: ASTD Press.

Zachary, L.J. 2000. *The Mentor's Guide*. San Francisco: John Wiley & Sons.

———. 2002. *Creating a Mentoring Culture: The Organization's Guide*. San Francisco: Jossey-Bass.

Zachary, L.J., and L.A. Fischler. 2010. "Those Who Lead, Mentor." *T+D*, March. www.td.org/Publications/Magazines/TD/TD-Archive/2010/03/Those-Who -Lead-Mentor.

# About the Author

Jenn Labin is the owner of T.E.R.P. associates, a team that seeks to grow talent and ignite potential. For 15 years, she has worked with a wide spectrum of organizations including large private-sector businesses, government and military operations, and higher-education institutions, specializing in implementing high-impact and high-value employee development solutions.

She has an extensive background in developing and facilitating content in mentoring and leadership programs. She also works with leadership development, DiSC and team communication, project management, change and innovation, mentoring and coaching, presentation design, performance management, and developing employees. Jenn helps individuals achieve greater potential through classroom training, workshops, long-term development programs, online modules, social media, presentations, and individual development plans. She partners with each client to uncover the unique needs and landscape before customizing solutions.

Jenn is also passionate about partnering with internal learning and development professionals to increase their expertise, influence, and impact. She is the author of *Real World Training Design*, a visual guide for creating exceptional results within tight budgets and timelines. Jenn co-authored a chapter on balancing time, quality, and expectations in the *ASTD Handbook*, 2nd Edition, and her whitepaper *5 Steps to Engagement: Simple and Practical Methods for Implementing an Employee Engagement Initiative* is one of three pieces she's published in *Pfeiffer Annual: Consulting*. Jenn's work can also be found in *101 Ways to Make Training Active, How to Write Terrific Training Materials*, and the ATD Trainer's Toolkit app. She presented at the ATD International Conference & EXPO in 2011 and 2015, as well as for local ATD chapters.

Jenn has a BA in digital art and an MA in instructional systems design from the University of Maryland, Baltimore County. She has earned credentials as a

Certified Principal Evaluator (Kirkpatrick Evaluation) and DISC-PIAV and Situational Leadership II Facilitator, as well as a certificate in presentation design from Duarte Design and Leadership Development. She is active at the national and local levels of ATD and has served on the ATD Press Editorial Advisory Board. Jenn is pursuing a coaching certification to expand her impact with senior leadership and executive partners. Besides learning and development, Jenn is passionate about scuba diving, the environment, and spending time with family. She lives near Baltimore, Maryland, with her amazing husband, daughters, and two turtles.

# About the Contributors

## Elaine Biech

Elaine Biech is president of ebb associates inc, a strategic implementation, leadership development, and experiential learning consulting firm. Elaine has been in the field for more than 30 years helping organizations work through large-scale change. She has presented at national and international conferences and has been featured in dozens of publications including the *Wall Street Journal, Harvard Management Update,* and *Fortune.* Elaine is the author and editor of more than 60 books, including *The Art and Science of Training; The ASTD Handbook,* 2nd edition; and *Training and Development for Dummies.* Elaine has received numerous awards including ATD's Bliss Award, Torch Award, and Staff Partnership Award. In 2012, she was the inaugural CPLP Fellow Program Honoree from the ATD Certification Institute. Elaine has served on ATD's board of directors and was the association secretary. She is currently a member of the Center for Creative Leadership Board of Governors and Berrett-Koehler's Worldwide Curator for the Advances in Leadership and Management Digital Collection.

## Kelly Irons

Kelly Irons launched developUs after more than a decade of consulting and project work while balancing a full-time job. As the founder and chief solutionist, Kelly brings a diverse background centered on a passion for performance improvement. Kelly has experience with recruitment and talent acquisition, team dynamics, sales CRM tools, and highly regulated government projects. Having held multiple leadership roles in large organizations, Kelly leverages her experience in nonprofit, private, and publicly held companies to create solutions that work given the company culture, values, and desired outcomes. She has a master's degree in training and organizational development and a bachelor's degree in psychology, is certified in multiple assessment tools and coaching programs, and has an Executive MBA certificate in talent management.

## Jim Kirkpatrick

Jim Kirkpatrick is a thought leader and change driver in training evaluation and the creator of the New World Kirkpatrick Model. Using his 15 years of experience in the corporate world, including eight years as a corporate training manager, Jim trains and consults for corporate, government, military, and humanitarian organizations around the world. He is passionate about assisting learning professionals in redefining themselves as strategic business partners to become a viable force in the workplace. Jim delivers lively keynote addresses and conducts workshops on topics including using evaluation to help execute business strategy, building and leveraging business partnerships, increasing the transfer of learning to on-the-job behaviors, and maximizing business results. Jim has co-written four books with Wendy Kirkpatrick, including *Kirkpatrick's Four Levels of Training Evaluation* and *Training on Trial*. They have also served as the subject matter experts for the United States Office of Personnel Management's *Training Evaluation Field Guide*.

## Wendy Kirkpatrick

Wendy is a global driving force of the use and implementation of the Kirkpatrick Model, leading companies to measurable success through training and evaluation. Wendy's results orientation stems from more than two decades of business experience in retailing, marketing, and training. She has held positions as a buyer, product manager, process manager, and training manager, which leveraged her ability to organize complex, multifaceted projects and yield rapid results. As a training manager, she managed the training curriculum for 1,500 sales and customer service representatives across North America. Wendy is a recipient of the 2013 Emerging Training Leaders Award from *Training* magazine. She has co-written four books with Jim Kirkpatrick, including *Kirkpatrick's Four Levels of Training Evaluation* and *Training on Trial*. They have also served as the subject matter experts for the United States Office of Personnel Management's *Training Evaluation Field Guide*.

## Jeanne Masseth

Jeanne has a passion for developing professional potential through mentoring. Her career spans 20 years of workplace learning expertise. As the CEO of Legacy Talent Development, Jeanne partners with clients to retain more engaged, effective employees. Her collaborative approach builds a road map of learning solutions with a laser focus on clients' unique business needs. She specializes in crafting talent strategy, building leaders, and sparking mentorship opportunities. As a lifelong learner and thought leader, Jeanne stays on the cutting edge of talent development to share trends and best practices with her clients. She holds a master's degree in business and has completed postgraduate work in educational leadership. Jeanne is certified as a mentoring facilitator and trainer, in addition to maintaining SPHR and SHRM-SCP designations.

## Michael Lee Stallard

Michael Lee Stallard speaks, teaches, and consults on leadership, employee engagement, organizational culture, productivity, and innovation. He is president of E Pluribus Partners; a co-founder of ConnectionCulture.com; author of *Connection Culture: The Competitive Advantage of Shared Identity, Empathy, and Understanding at Work* and *Fired Up or Burned Out: How to Reignite Your Team's Passion, Productivity, and Creativity*; and a contributor to *The ASTD Management Development Handbook*. Articles written by Michael or about his work have appeared in leadership periodicals worldwide. He has spoken or taught at many leading organizations, including General Electric, Google, Johnson & Johnson, the M.D. Anderson Cancer Center, the NASA Johnson Space Center, Scotiabank, the U.S. Treasury Department, and the Yale-New Haven Hospital.

## Jean Williams

Jean Williams, founder of Williams Consulting Group, has more than 20 years' experience in executive and leadership development and general management. She spent 10 years as a management consultant, working for many of the most recognized companies in the world, including Cisco, eBay, PayPal, Chevron, Fidelity Investments, Boston Scientific, DuPont, Ford Motor Company, United Technologies, Federated Department Stores, and AT&T. Jean is an experienced facilitator and a certified executive coach, and has led innumerable leadership, management, marketing, strategy, and sales training programs. Her specialties include designing and delivering training programs, particularly focused on leadership and strategy, executive coaching, design and facilitation of strategy sessions, working virtually, and employee engagement. Jean has an MBA from Northwestern University's Kellogg School of Management and a BA in history and theater from Connecticut College.

## Lois Zachary

Lois Zachary is an internationally recognized expert in mentoring. Her bestselling books, *The Mentor's Guide, Creating a Mentoring Culture,* and most recently, *The Mentee's Guide,* have become primary resources for Fortune 500 companies, as well as government, education, technology, healthcare, and nonprofit organizations interested in promoting mentoring for leadership and learning. Lois is the president of Leadership Development Services, a Phoenix-based consulting firm that specializes in leadership and mentoring, and is the director of its Center for Mentoring Excellence. She has been recognized as one of the top 100 minds in leadership and has published more than 100 articles on the topics of leadership and mentoring. Lois holds two master's degrees and earned a doctorate in adult and continuing education from Teachers College Columbia University. She is a founding member and past chairperson of the Phoenix Athena PowerLink Governing Board, which helps women-owned businesses expand profitably through the use of mentoring advisory panels.

# Index